Table of Contents

The Sacraments Today

Their Meaning and Celebration

Christopher Farrell, C.SS.R.
and
Thomas Artz, C.SS.R.

LIGUORI
PUBLICATIONS

One Liguori Drive
Liguori, Missouri 63057
(314) 464-2500

Imprimi Potest:
Edmund T. Langton, C.SS.R.
Provincial, St. Louis Province
Redemptorist Fathers

Imprimatur:
+ John N. Wurm, S.T.D., Ph.D.
Vicar General, Archdiocese of St. Louis
ISBN 0-89243-087-7
Copyright © 1978, Liguori Publications
Printed in U. S. A.
Library of Congress Catalog Card Number: 78-069750

Cover design: Linda Harris

Photo credits:
Blahusch: pp. 28, 54, 110, 130
Ebenhoh: pp. 76, 94

ACKNOWLEDGMENTS
The following Liguori Publications pamphlets form the
basis of this book. Each one has been revised and expanded
to form the complete whole which appears here.

Sacraments: Signs of Love
  Christopher Farrell, C.SS.R.

Preparing for the Baptism of Your Child
  Rev. Nicholas Schneider

Confirmation: What It Is and What It Does
  Thomas Artz, C.SS.R.

Eucharist: Center of Christian Life
  Rod Kissinger, S.J.

What You Should Know About the
Sacrament of Penance
  Christopher Farrell, C.SS.R.

The Anointing of the Sick
  John Steingraeber, C.SS.R.

Matrimony: Sacrament of Christian Love
  Thomas Artz, C.SS.R.

Holy Orders: Sacrament of Priesthood
  Thomas Artz, C.SS.R.

Introduction

The title for this book has been chosen with deliberate care. These pages contain a treatment of the sacraments whose rites have been revised according to the directions of the Second Vatican Council. Our concern is the basic meaning or understanding of the sacraments in general and each one in particular. Our purpose is to motivate readers to a meaningful celebration of them, instead of a merely mechanical performance.

The main objective of the present-day ritual changes in the celebration of the sacraments is to help us realize that ours is a sacramental existence. Christ is the center and source of life. He is the great Sacrament in whom the Father reveals his design for all people to transform them into the same image. The Church too is a perpetual sacrament without which we would be unable to celebrate the seven sacraments. And the sacraments themselves help us to discover God's saving presence in all of creation, especially in the human persons he created to his own image and likeness. To each other, then, we become a kind of sacrament, a visible sign of Christ's redeeming love. The ritual changes in the sacramental system are meant to bring out more clearly the significance and spiritual wealth of the sacraments.

We learn to appreciate this spiritual wealth when we come to understand how the sacraments fit into our personal and communal history of salvation. Ours is the age of the sacraments; we live in the interval between the first and second coming of Christ. But we should not think of them primarily as means of salvation or as external aids to help us carry out a law which has already been given. They are themselves a joyous proclamation of the decisive law of Christians, the "law of grace," and they bring all of God's commandments into their proper place within this law. They are signs of God's fidelity to us. And when we are faithful in receiving them — because we know their meaning — they become the law of our lives. To live a truly Christian life, then, depends on our understanding of the sacraments.

The sacraments as visible signs of an invisible grace are divine encounters with Christ. They are received personally, but each one has a communal aspect that has not always been appreciated in the past. They are community celebrations of the mysteries of salvation. Many of us, however, have grown up in an atmosphere of spiritual individualism. We see each sacrament as a personal encounter with Christ — which it is — but the new ritual celebration of the sacraments recalls the social or communal aspect of all the sacraments. The liturgical services — by which the sacraments are imparted — are not private functions. They are celebrations of the Church — the People of God. This is why the *Constitution on the Liturgy* stresses active participation of the laity. They are encouraged to participate by means of acclamations, responses, and songs, as well as by actions, gestures, and bodily attitudes. Our meaningful celebration of the sacraments will eliminate any formalism and routine that have perhaps plagued us in the past.

The overall purpose of this book, then, is to develop in the reader a sense of sacramental practicality. This means that liturgical piety in the celebration of the sacraments will consciously lead to the use of God's gift of grace for benefit of self and others.

Father Bernard Häring in his book *The Sacraments and Your Everyday Life* refers to this in his Introduction. He chooses the Eucharist to make his point. He quotes the Offertory prayer on the feast of Corpus Christi, ". . . may the bread and cup we offer bring your Church the unity and peace they signify."

He then continues: "This unity and solidarity of the people of the New Covenant are not meant to remain invisible, mysterious effects of Eucharistic grace. Symbolically and perceptibly, the sacraments express God's gift and call to unity and peace. Obviously, then, it is incongruous for confessors and preachers to insist that the faithful assist at the Eucharist in parishes where unity and solidarity are nonexistent, where the liturgy fails to invite it in any visible way.

"Think of a parish that accepts racial discrimination with no effort of conversion. Christians cannot truly participate in the Eucharistic celebration unless they perceive and accept the message and the grace of the sacrament as norms of unity and solidarity. If in the whole life of the parish there is little or practically no concern for fostering these Christian and human attitudes, the lack becomes, by necessity, strikingly evident in its way of worshiping. Of what use, then, is it to assert the doctrine that the Eucharist is the sacrament of unity if there is no visible and effective bond uniting people, and if the cult does not change our life for the better? What good is sacramental activity if it does not increase in the participants that unity before God which would make them operators of peace, reconciliation, and unity in the world?"

These questions will not arise when Catholics learn to see the intimate connection between liturgy and life. And that is our purpose here: to provide the necessary knowledge about the sacraments and to promote a meaningful celebration of them. The sacraments are not just "things to be done" on an occasional basis; they are graces to be lived every day of our lives.

Chapter 1
Sacraments:
Seven Special Signs

If everyone knew what the sacraments were and how to celebrate them meaningfully, this book would not be necessary. However, this is not the case.

At the recommendation of the Fathers gathered at the Second Vatican Council, new dimensions of the sacraments are presently being emphasized and different rites have now been prescribed. Children must be taught. Teen-agers need to know as they grow. Adults, too, must understand the importance of these seven special elements of their faith-life. Even priests and Sisters must call to mind the value of the sacraments and their place in everyone's Christian life.

We should all strive to know what the sacraments are and what they are not, what they can do for us and what we must do to receive them. First we must look to the sacraments in general, and then to each sacrament in particular.

We can begin by trying to end one common misunderstanding that has been a problem for many years. It is a disturbing fact that many people today look on the Church as a huge supermarket.

For material things this modern convenience is great. Choose your own cart. Wheel it down the well-marked aisles. Pick out what you want. Line up at the check-out counter. Watch as the items mount. Pay your bill; and you are on your way — your temporal needs for the moment taken care of.

When your supplies are exhausted you run out for more of the same. And back again, you go through the same routine. Choose, wheel, pick out, line up, watch and pay. There may be a variety in your needs, but there is a definite sameness about the whole procedure.

But the church is not just a place where people go from time to time to take care of their spiritual needs. The priest is not just a clerk who advises them about certain items in stock; and even — like the delivery boy of the corner grocery store — brings them special orders when they cannot come themselves. And the sacraments are not just spiritual stockpiles reserved for special crises in their lives.

Of course, these are extreme attitudes. But they cannot be denied. Just press the right button or know the right man, and you are automatically saved. There is nothing personal about it at all. And when Christ is mentioned he seems only a vague personality who lived centuries ago. He is not seen as someone who loves me here and now.

HOW THESE ATTITUDES DEVELOPED

No doubt the Church herself is responsible for some of these attitudes. But when God spoke to and made promises to his chosen race he was not impersonal. "I will remember my covenant which is between me and you and every living creature of all flesh" (Gn 9:15). During his lifetime Christ established a personal relationship between himself, his apostles, and his people. "If you abide in me, and if my words abide in you, ask whatever you will and it shall be done to you" (Jn 15:7). And the Church which Christ founded maintained that familiar approach through the early centuries of her existence.

However, as the world expanded and the faith spread, the Church experienced the same difficulty that every organization must face. She grew from a small seed to a full-grown tree, but at the same time she began to lose her personal touch.

Now this did not happen overnight. When Church persecutions came to an end, people had more time to study the teachings of Christ. Their purpose was to understand them better and to develop them further. It was enough for the early Christians — fighting for their existence — to believe in the basic doctrine of the Trinity, for example. But further study gave us a deeper insight into this mystery by exploring the relationship of the three Persons.

We owe much to the schoolmen (the scholastics) of the Middle Ages — men like St. Thomas Aquinas and others; because of their tireless effort the implications of God's Word became better known. These men, however, belonged to the educated class; and the vast majority of the ordinary people — who could not afford to attend a university — remained uneducated. As a result many of them centered on the personalities of the medieval Church rather than the person of Christ. They began to see the Church as an institution with merely human rules and regulations instead of a community who gathered together as the People of God.

The Renaissance and the Reformation brought on further complications. The humanistic approach became almost too human. And when Martin Luther broke with his Church the reaction was more than human. Today, the Church admits that many of his reforms were quite legitimate; but in reacting to his rebellion she felt that she dare not give ground on any point. Thus, the Counter Reformation came into being as a form of rebuttal rather than a positive presentation of Christ's teachings.

ENCOUNTERING CHRIST

Among others, Martin Luther saw what was happening. He felt that religion should be more personalized, that Christ should be approached as a Man who was God, rather than a God who became Man. Thus, in the beginning — before it got out of control — the Reformation was meant to be a return to Christ as a personal Savior. And this indeed he was in his own time and in the early Church.

No doubt, religion had become rather impersonal, even mechanistic, in Luther's time. And he was right in demanding reform. But, just as the Council of Trent seemed to lean over backward rather than admit that Luther might be right in certain points, so the reformers began to throw overboard doctrines of the Church which they had originally held sacred.

In many ways, then, Luther was good for the Church; he reminded her of the necessity of reform. And the Council of Trent — despite the difficulties of the time — performed commendably. Its task was, in a certain sense, like that of Vatican II in our own time: to return to original sources and to center more on the person of Christ while cutting away some of the nonessential trappings. It defined the sacraments, for example, as communicators of God's saving grace to Christians. It decreed the language of worship to be Latin, but nowhere did it condemn the theoretical use of the vernacular.

Today, it is easy enough for us to criticize our ancestors. But we live in a pluralistic society established by the traumatic experience they had to face. And, like Monday morning quarterbacks, we can see the mistakes made by both sides in the controversy. However, the problem still exists in our modern times and that is why the post-conciliar directions concerning the liturgy have been written: to help us see more clearly the meaning behind the sacramental signs.

Our understanding of the new directions will depend very much on the way we approach (encounter) Christ in the sacraments.

We may approach him as the Man who was God — realizing that the same love he showed the people of his time is being extended to us today. And because of this personal experience of Christ we will go on to an understanding of his power and glory, his justice and his mercy. Or, we may approach him as the Son of his Father who is infinitely perfect, eternal, all-knowing, etc. And this powerful and exciting knowledge of God prepares us for our personal encounter with Christ as he exists in his Mystical Body, the Church.

Now both of the above methods of encountering Christ are good in themselves. It is the latter approach, however, that was prevalent at the time of the Reformation. And looking back we can see how it was possible for Catholics of that day to view Christ and his sacraments in a mechanical way.

FAITH IN CHRIST

We encounter Christ in faith, but faith in him can be experienced in different ways. I can *know* my faith as an object of my belief — broken down into its essential parts so as to be better understood. But the danger here is that I remain satisfied with this mere knowledge and never actually go on to *love* the person of Christ. Or, my faith can begin by loving the person of Christ, and because of this love, come to a fuller understanding of his power, mercy, justice, etc. The danger here is that I may make my love too subjective. Not knowing what justice is, for example, I may be guilty of crimes against it — all in the name of love. Thus, there is danger in both approaches. Each must follow through — from love to knowledge, or from knowledge to love. But in either case, my faith must consist in my individual response to Christ's personal love.

With this understanding of the different ways of encountering Christ, what is the best way to approach Christ in his sacraments today?

HISTORY OF SALVATION

To answer this question satisfactorily we must learn to appreciate what is called the history of salvation.

Briefly, it is the story of God's love for man. In the Old Testament we see the divine plan of redemption unfold. God calls Abraham and he generously responds. Under Moses the family of Abraham is welded together as a people by means of a covenant — a pact of loyalty which God's people fulfill by obedience to his commandments. Joshua then led them to the promised land of Palestine. This land becomes a kingdom; and the name forever associated with it is that of David. After their exile in Babylon the People of God return under the leadership of Ezra to form a community of worshipers in the rebuilt Temple. Thus God worked with his people — calling, saving, strengthening, forgiving. They responded, relapsed, and returned. And all the time they looked forward to the coming of the Messiah, the Redeemer.

After centuries of waiting that Redeemer arrived in the person of Christ. He came not to abolish the law and the prophets . . . but to fulfill them, that is, to reveal their true meaning and extent. With his birth, death and Resurrection, as told in the four Gospels, began the Messianic era. It will continue until his Second Coming in clouds of glory.

The Acts of the Apostles and the Epistles continue the story of our salvation. These infant years of the Church show Christ living in the world, doing now through his Mystical Body what he had done in Palestine through his physical body.

We then are a continuation of that saving history. Christ remains with us as the Way, the Truth and the Life. And it is his life that comes to us in the sacraments. They are seven special signs of his love by which we share in his divine life.

WHAT IS A SACRAMENT?

Before Christ died, he himself was a living sacrament to the People of God. He shared his divine life with them. To the woman who anointed his feet, he said: "Your sins are forgiven" (Lk 7:48). Today, we too are in divine contact with him through the sacraments of his Mystical Body, the Church.

Gradually through the centuries the sacraments were defined. They came to be known as signs instituted by Christ to give us grace. The key words have always been "Christ," "sign," and "grace."

Instituted by Christ

Christ *immediately* instituted all the sacraments of the New Law. This means that he laid down once and for all the essential elements of each sacrament. It does not mean that he spelled out every little detail as to how each rite is to be performed. For example, Baptism has been administered through the centuries by immersion or by pouring water on the head of the person being baptized. Christ himself told Nicodemus, "Unless a man be born again of water and the Spirit, he cannot enter the kingdom of God" (Jn 3:5). And for this reason he told the apostles to go forth to all nations "baptizing them in the name of the Father, and of the Son, and of the Holy Spirit" (Mt 28:19).

Just as Christ is the focal point of salvation history, so too he is the center of the sacraments. He established them and he is the divine guarantee that they give us a share in his divine life *as he promised.* Without Christ, the sacraments are but empty ceremonies. We have always known this, but — as we have seen — people began to stress the ceremonies more than the person of Christ.

Today, in order to restore proper balance the Church is reemphasizing the person of Christ.

Signs

Christ did the most natural thing in the world when he chose as his signs material things that were familiar to everyone. He had taught the people by means of stories. They knew what he meant when he spoke of seed sown in the ground; and of trees with good and bad fruit. They understood when he talked about vines and branches. In much the same way he made use of similar actions and things when he created the sacred things we call the sacraments. Water cleansed. Bread and wine satisfied hunger and thirst. Oil preserved. These facts they knew.

He told his apostles that his love would remain with them through the use of these signs. They had faith in his divine words. So, they used water and called on the name of the Trinity to cleanse the soul from sin and lead it from death to life. They spoke the words he bade them speak at the Last Supper and ordinary bread and wine became the body and blood of the Savior — to cause divine growth in the person who ate and drank of it. They anointed with oil and called on the Holy Spirit to preserve the soul and body of the person thus anointed. And so with all the sacraments.

That outward signs may indicate inward changes should not seem strange to us. In cap and gown, a young lady steps forward to receive her university diploma. Yesterday she struggled to learn; tomorrow she begins to teach. The cap, the gown, and the diploma are external symbols of a change in status. From learner she has advanced to teacher. A young boy, after due preparation, stands before his bishop to be anointed with oil — a symbol of strength — and signed with the sign of the cross. Facing the bishop, he was a child of God. Returning to his place, he is a witness to Jesus Christ. Yes, actions and words do convey meanings to us even when we can see no external or outward change.

As human beings we express our attitudes mainly by physical actions. Friendship, though a matter of heart and mind, is expressed through the body. While Christ was on earth he made himself known through his human nature; today he operates through his Mystical Body, the Church. When he shows friendship, or love, for us in his sacraments he gives fully of himself. But our responses will vary, according to the intensity of our love or friendship.

This explains why in receiving the sacraments some continue to grow in their love of Christ, while others drift away. It is the difference between loving and unloving commitment to Christ.

Grace

These signs, symbols or ceremonies are Christ's way of giving us grace or increasing it within us. Grace has always been a mysterious word. We are familiar with the word "gracious" which means "kind," and the word "graceful" which means "attractive." And when we speak of "the grace of God," we refer both to God's kindly attitude toward us and the divine effect it has on us.

As a sign of God's love each sacrament is a gift of his grace. Because he is gracious he makes us graceful. And the effects on us are astounding. "If anyone loves me, he will keep my word, and my Father will love him, and we shall come to him and make our abode with him" (Jn 14:23).

The inspired writers when speaking of what we call "grace" were more interested in appreciation than definition. But at times we seem more concerned with our definitions and analogies of grace than our appreciation of it. It is not some kind of "spiritual liquid" that God pours into our soul. Grace is divine life within us. Through the grace of Baptism, for example, we become children of God and heirs of heaven. Grace may come and go; we can accept God's love, or refuse it. To remain in the state of grace means that our union, our friendship with God is still intimate.

To appreciate this friendship, comparisons do help — as long as we do not substitute them for the real thing. The relationship between God and ourselves is somewhat like the understanding that exists between two people who love each other deeply. Each comes to know — almost instinctively — what the other needs, wants and loves. God has always had this understanding of us. And we will share in that understanding by a loving use of the sacraments.

Because grace is a bond of friendship between God and us, the sacraments "give grace" in the sense that they are signs which express this friendship. They not only "contain grace" but they actually express God's gracious love for us and our loving response to him.

MINISTERS OF THE SACRAMENTS

All grace comes from God alone, because he alone can freely make a human being his adopted child. It comes to us through Jesus. "God is one. One also is the mediator between God and men, the man Christ Jesus, who gave himself as a ransom for all" (1 Tm 2:5).

Christ comes to us through Word (Scripture) and sacrament — both of which are in the loving care of the Church. Centuries ago St. Cyprian wrote: "No one can have God for Father who does not have the Church for mother." Regrettably, some see the Church as a stern father concerned only with making and enforcing rules and regulations. But she is truly a loving mother who, in the person of the apostles, received the commission to administer the sacraments.

Necessarily, then, the ministers of the sacraments will be human beings who make up the body of the Church. The ordinary ministers are bishops and priests. However, in case of emergency, anyone (as long as he/she intends to do what the Church does) may baptize. Also, in the marriage ceremony the bride and groom administer the sacrament to each other, the priest acting as the official witness of the Church.

When we receive the sacraments worthily we do not identify ourselves with the minister of those sacraments. Rather, we identify with Christ whom the minister represents. This is our contact with him. Thus begins our involvement. And the grace which Christ gives us in response to that involvement causes us to commit ourselves entirely to him. The end result will be that we begin to think Christ, talk Christ, and act Christ.

PERSONAL APPROACH

Today, as we have seen, many Catholics look at the sacraments in a mechanistic sort of way. To them a sacrament is a thing (or series of actions) which in a mysterious way does something wonderful to their individual souls. Each sacrament is a procedure to which they submit themselves; and they feel that something magical has taken place within them because they have submitted themselves to this automatic process.

But the sacraments are not just things or actions outside of us. They are personal experiences or happenings in our lives. Because of this, proper preparation for reception is necessary. To receive Communion in the state of mortal sin, to confess mortal sins with no intention of avoiding them as best as possible in the future — these are examples of a lack of preparation. They are mockeries of Christ.

Even more necessary is full cooperation with God's gift of grace after a sacrament has been received. Each sacrament creates a resemblance to Christ which is to be manifested in daily life, and a special grace is given for this purpose. Thus the sacraments authentically understood and lived are the foundation and the norm of all spiritual life. (See the Epistles of St. Paul.)

Each sacrament sets up an interpersonal relationship between Christ and Christian. It is difficult to explain how this takes place, but perhaps a comparison will give us an indication. We have all been stirred from within at times. We recognize the spirit that somehow takes hold of us when our home team makes an outstanding play — causing us to stand up and cheer. We have felt the rhythm that makes us tap our feet and sway our bodies when we hear good music.

On these occasions we somehow become one with the player. We, in spirit, are hitting that home run, scoring that touchdown, beating out that tempo. We do not physically exchange places with the other person, but there is between us a living link — a link that joins us invisibly.

WHY THE PERSONAL APPROACH?

That we should return to this personal approach to the sacraments should be clear from a reading of history and an examination of our natural instincts.

Before the industrial revolution, people exercised great personal freedom. They planned and did their work personally. Their wants were few and they spent more time than money at their daily occupations. As a result, much of that work was truly personal and therefore artistic.

But modern civilization has changed all this. Machines in many cases have taken over for man himself; computers do much of his brain work. In hospitals, doctors and nurses care for "the appendix" in Room 203, or "the heart" in Room 109. Social workers refer to Case No. 63. In almost all fields of activity man is being depersonalized.

But, all is not lost. Did you ever notice how easily a child grows tired of his machine-perfect toy and goes back to his beat-up plaything — perhaps a rag doll that grandma made? Even adults will caress with their hands, or at least with their eyes, a handmade work of art — preferring it to a machine-made product.

Doubtless the reason for all this is that no two homemade objects are alike. Each artist does things in a different way. There is a personal element here that we can never find in a machine-perfect product.

This personal approach to things and people seems to be a part of our human nature. Thus history and human nature remind us that we must approach the sacraments person to Person. Our salvation — individual and corporate — depends upon it.

SENSE OF COMMUNITY

Each sacrament is received individually because the friendship of God is something personal. However, we must not lose sight of the community aspect of the sacraments. I am responsible for my personal commitment to Christ; I must save myself as a person — body and soul. Yet, I am not an isolated stone in the building of God's Church. As a social being, I am a member of a community — my home, my neighborhood, my Church. All my actions therefore have a definite effect on others.

When I receive the sacraments, the commitment I make is not just an individual one — between Christ and myself. Since these signs of grace are signs of the Church, the sacraments are given in the community and for the sake of the community. Their purpose is to build up the Church — all the members of the Mystical Body of Christ. Through them the Church manifests itself. For example, around the Eucharist Christians gather every Sunday as around the family table, an essential action of communal life. And so with all the sacraments — each in its own way emphasizes sanctification and salvation as a community affair.

My loving response to God flows from me to God's people. And thus begins a never-ending relationship — as long as I continue to respond to God's love. God extends his love to me. I accept. But since his limitless love cannot be contained within my limited being, it influences my personal relationships with others. This same process is going on in each member of the community — with the result that we all love each other because of the love of God in our own hearts. And it is the sacraments that maintain this flow of love.

SEVEN SACRAMENTS

There are seven sacraments of the New Law, and only seven, all of them instituted by our Savior. This was clearly stated by the Council of Trent. The number could easily be six — by combining Baptism and Confirmation. Or it could be nine — by expanding Holy Orders to deacon-priest-bishop.

Why seven, and only seven? Many reasons have been given, but one of the more plausible explanations is the following: Our search for salvation consists of a pilgrimage much like that of the Hebrews through the desert between the crossing of the Red Sea and the crossing of the Jordan. The stages of our journey correspond somewhat to the stages of that original journey. Christ intervenes in our behalf at these various points. In this way the personal history of each Christian is made part of the history of salvation itself.

Thus the Church reverently compares the seven sacraments to bodily and social life.

Through Baptism we are *born* into the Mystical Body of Christ so that with him we are children of God.

Through Confirmation we become mature enough to exert a social influence on the world as witnesses to Christ.

Through Holy Eucharist we are fed with Christ, the Bread of Life, in a community banquet.

Through Penance we are revitalized, if our sins have weakened or killed our friendship with Christ and our fellow human beings.

Through the Anointing of the Sick we regain health or gain strength from Christ to pass through death into eternal life.

In Holy Orders priests are chosen to preach the Good News, form communities and administer the sacraments which activate Christ's love for the People of God.

In Matrimony, partners are chosen by one another to live a life of responsible love which mirrors within the family circle Christ's love for his Church.

The sacraments are not supermarket specials. They are true signs of love between God and man. Every sacrament is a personal meeting with Christ. We make our original commitment to him at Baptism. From that moment on our friendship with God (and therefore with our neighbors) either increases or decreases. There is no standing still, because love is active. Love must grow, or it will die.

This personal approach to the sacraments should make us not only *know* our faith but *live* it. We must look on them not just as ceremonies (or things) that make us holy but as divine encounters which draw loving responses from us, so that we freely commit ourselves to a friendship that will never die. If we make use of the sacraments in this personal way, then our lives will be truly Christ-centered.

SACRAMENTS OF INITIATION

Baptism:
Entrance into Christ's Church

Eucharist:
Center of Christian Life

Confirmation:
Filled With the Spirit

Baptism, Confirmation and Eucharist are called the sacraments of initiation. As was customary in the early Church, the bishop conferred them on adults in immediate succession. In the Eastern rites this is still the rule, even for infants. Adult converts today now have the opportunity of receiving them in the same way as the early Christians. (We will give a brief summary of this rite called "Christian Initiation of Adults" in our chapter on Baptism.)

Since the majority of Catholics in our time are baptized as infants, the order of reception of these sacraments does differ in the Western (Roman) Church. But the fact remains that initiation is not really complete until Baptism is followed by Confirmation and Eucharist. For this reason the Church has decreed that the latter two be given to children at an early age, as soon as she judges them ready. And in the revised rite for Confirmation the baptismal promises are renewed before the reception of this sacrament.

Baptism is called "the sacrament of faith." With it we become a part of the family of God and by it we become adopted sons and daughters of God. Without it we cannot receive any of the other sacraments of the Church. Freed from sin by its cleansing waters, it is the basis of all Christian life. It may end a journey — sometimes a very lengthy one — that has brought a person to Christ; or it may begin a journey with Christ to the Father. From it Christian spirituality flows. Down through the ages the impulse to religious life, to the perfection of the Gospel, to the apostolate has sprung from a renewed realization of the implications of Baptism.

Confirmation is closely related to Baptism but distinct from it. It "completes" or "perfects" Baptism. When we are confirmed we become "perfect" in the sense that we have attained, on the sacramental plane, the fullness of likeness to Christ. Reborn at Baptism, we reach maturity in Confirmation. These two sacraments, then, are complementary. At Baptism we are marked with the baptismal character, the indelible sign of Christ. At Confirmation we receive the character of prophet and witness to Christ. And the grace proper to Baptism differs from that of Confirmation. The Holy Spirit is given at Baptism; without him there would be no remission of sins and no grace. The second giving of the Spirit in Confirmation comes to us in view of our public mission as Christians to be witnesses and messengers of Christ.

The Eucharist followed Baptism and Confirmation in the ancient liturgy. All the baptized received Communion, whether they were adults or little children (the latter received only the species of wine). This bond between Baptism and the Eucharist consists in the unity of the paschal mystery. Baptism draws its efficacy from the sacrifice of Christ which the Eucharist makes present. Baptism incorporates us into Christ; the body of Christ is given us as food to seal our union with him. Baptism opens out to us the road to the Promised Land, and the Eucharist is the anticipation and pledge of our inheritance of this land. Our preparation for first Communion — whether as a young child or as an adult convert — should therefore emphasize the fact that we now begin to take a full part in the Mass as members of the priestly People of God. Seen in this perspective of Christian initiation, Communion is not an isolated act; it is a beginning, not an end in itself.

Thus, in these three sacraments of initiation we are reborn as the sons and daughters of God, we become mature witnesses of Christ in the Spirit, and we are nourished by the body and blood of Christ himself.

Chapter 2
Baptism:
Entrance into Christ's Church

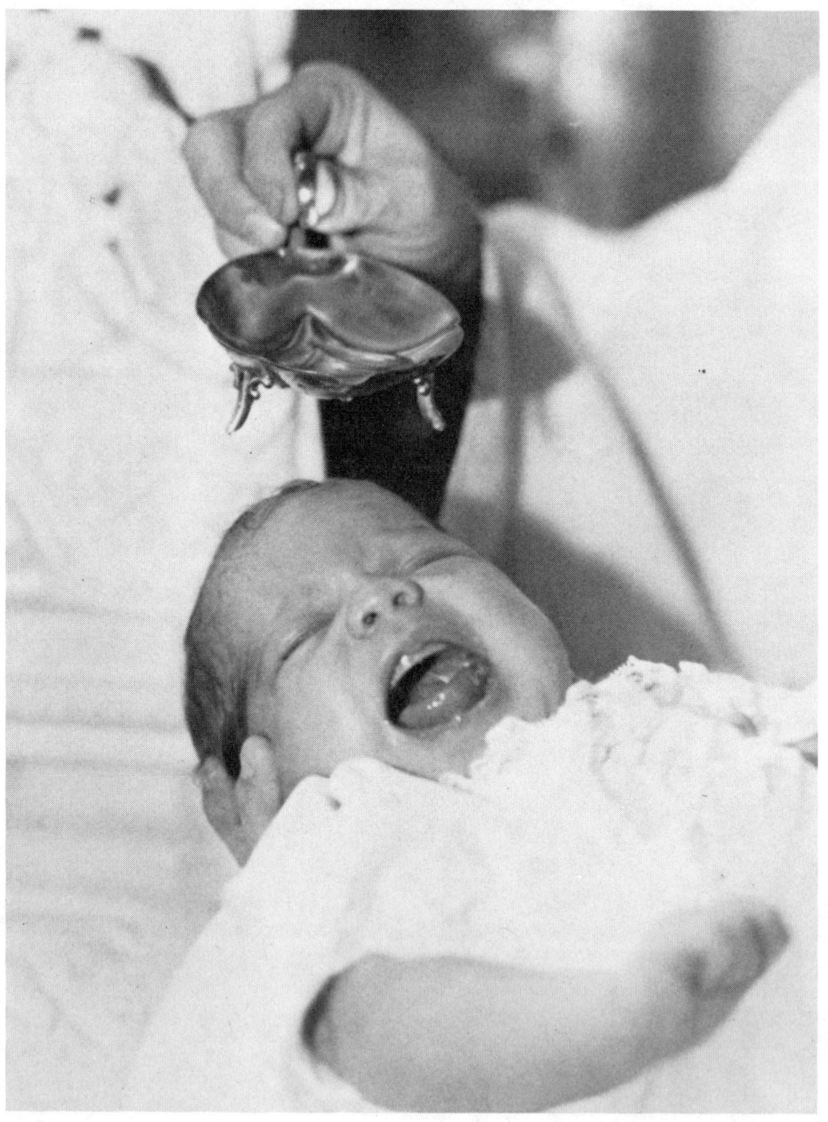

I
A CELEBRATION OF THE CHURCH

To become a Christian and a member of the Church we must receive faith and Baptism. Baptism and faith are, in fact, so closely united that Baptism is called "the sacrament of faith." But Baptism cannot be understood without the other two sacraments closely connected with it — Confirmation and the Eucharist. Confirmation completes and perfects Baptism. The Eucharist is the family table to which Baptism gives access. Although adult initiation into these three sacraments is naturally a more meaningful commitment — since it takes place at a later age — Baptism of children is now considered the norm and these pages will concern themselves mainly with the children's rite.

Here we will explain the effects of Baptism on those who receive it, and also address those who participate in the sacrament as parents and godparents.

Of course, adults preparing for Baptism can learn from what is written here, but our main purpose is to remind parents and godparents of their serious responsibilities in this area.

A SACRAMENT OF THE CHURCH

Baptism is the door to life and to the kingdom of God. Christ offered this first sacrament of the New Law to all men that they might have eternal life. He entrusted Baptism and the Gospel to his Church when he told his apostles: "Go, make disciples of all nations, and baptize them in the name of the Father, and of the Son, and of the Holy Spirit."

Therefore, Baptism is the sacrament of faith by which we, enlightened by the Spirit's grace, respond to the Gospel of Christ. That is why the Church believes it her most basic and necessary duty to inspire all — catechumens (those preparing to be baptized), parents and godparents — to that true and living faith by which they adhere to Christ and enter into or confirm their commitment to the New Covenant. She does this by her pastoral instruction of catechumens and by the careful preparation of parents and godparents as described here.

Through Baptism we are incorporated into the Church and become members of a holy nation and therefore children of God, sharing in Christ's own royal and priestly dignity. Baptism creates a sacramental bond of unity linking all who have been signed by it. Because of its indelible character (signified in the liturgy by the anointing with chrism), the rite of Baptism is held in highest honor by all Christians. It may never lawfully be repeated once it has been validly celebrated.

Baptism makes us sharers in God's own life and his adopted children. We are prepared for this high dignity and led into it by scriptural readings, the prayer of the community, and the three-fold profession of faith. Purified by the water of rebirth and consecrated in the name of the Trinity, we enter into fellowship with the Father, the Son, and the Holy Spirit.

BAPTISM AND THE PASCHAL MYSTERY

Far superior to the purifications of the Old Law, Baptism is empowered with the mystery of the Lord's Passion and Resurrection. We who are baptized are engrafted in the likeness of Christ's death. We are buried with him, given life again with him, and with him we rise again. For Baptism recalls and effects the paschal mystery itself, because by means of it we pass from the death of sin into the life of God. Its celebration, therefore, should reflect the joy of the Resurrection, especially when it takes place during the Easter Vigil or on Sunday.

GROWING TO MATURITY IN CHRIST

Baptism is the first of the three sacraments of Christian initiation. Through it we are incorporated into Christ and obtain forgiveness of our sins. We become a new creation through water and the Holy Spirit.

Confirmation then signs us with the gift of the Spirit and fills us with that same Spirit. Thus strengthened, we can bear witness to our Lord before all the world and eagerly work to build up the Body of Christ.

In due time we come to the table of the Eucharist to eat the flesh and drink the blood of the Son of Man so that we may have eternal life and show forth the unity of God's people. By offering ourselves with Christ, we share in his universal sacrifice; the entire community of the redeemed is offered to God by their high priest. We also pray for a greater outpouring of the Holy Spirit so that the whole human race may be brought into the unity of God's family.

Thus Baptism, Confirmation, and the Eucharist together bring us to full maturity in Christ and enable us to carry out our mission as the People of God in the Church and in the world.

CHRISTIAN INITIATION OF ADULTS

Those who are preparing to receive these three sacraments of initiation are called catechumens. During their period of instruction and formation they now have special rites or ceremonies to aid them at various stages in their conversion. (Formerly, most converts merely received a course of instructions and then were baptized immediately.)

Their journey takes place in the midst of the community of the faithful, who by their example lead the catechumens to obey the Holy Spirit more generously. They progress through three stages:

a) At the point of initial conversion, they express their wish to become Christians and are accepted as catechumens by the Church.

b) When their faith has grown and their instruction is almost completed, they are admitted to a more profound preparation for the sacraments.

c) After their spiritual preparation is completed, they receive the three sacraments of initiation.

For each of these stages there is a special rite or ceremony: Rite of Becoming Catechumens; Rite of Election or Enrollment of Names; and Celebration of the Sacraments of Initiation.

The Christian initiation described above is intended for adults. In the following pages we will deal primarily with infant Baptism since it is much more common.

SPECIAL CEREMONY FOR CHILDREN

Strange as it may seem, until Vatican Council II there had never been a rite of Baptism specifically for children in the entire history of the Church. The first initiates to the faith were adults and a rite of Baptism was drawn up for them. When children were baptized, the rite was somewhat adjusted for this purpose, but it remained basically orientated to its original usage as a rite for adults. For this reason the bishops at Vatican Council II directed that the rite be revised and adapted to form a definite rite for infants. They further requested that the rite bring out more clearly the roles and duties of parents and godparents. With the issuance of the new Rite of Baptism for Children on May 15, 1969, the Congregation for Divine Worship achieved this task.

II
A FAMILY CELEBRATION

IMPORTANCE OF BAPTIZING CHILDREN

From the earliest times the Church, to which the mission of preaching the Gospel and baptizing was entrusted, has baptized children as well as adults. Our Lord said: "Unless a man is reborn in water and the Holy Spirit, he cannot enter the kingdom of God." The Church has always understood these words to include children as well as adults. Although infants cannot profess the faith they receive at Baptism, the Church supplies for them. Their faith is proclaimed for them by their parents and godparents, who represent both the local Church and the whole society of saints and believers: "The Church is at once the mother of all and the mother of each."

To fulfill the true meaning of the sacrament, children must later be formed in the faith in which they have been baptized. The foundation of this formation will be the sacrament itself, which they have already received. It is the duty of parents and/or godparents to see that this Christian formation takes place. If, while they are young, they gradually learn God's plan for them in Christ, they will ultimately accept for themselves the faith in which they have been baptized.

WHEN TO CELEBRATE BAPTISM

The spiritual welfare of the offspring must take first consideration; the child must not be deprived of Baptism. The health of the mother must also be considered, since she should be present when the sacrament is celebrated. Also, sufficient time should be allowed for parents and godparents to properly prepare themselves for baptismal celebration.

a) As soon as possible, and even before the child is born, the parish priest should be informed so that the proper preparations can be made.

b) In danger of death, the child should be baptized without delay.

c) Otherwise, the infant should be baptized within the first weeks after birth.

HOW TO CELEBRATE BAPTISM

Immediate Preparations:

a) Make arrangements with the parish priest concerning the date and time of the Baptism.

b) Choose the godparents and invite relatives and friends to the celebration.

c) Select a Christian name for the child.

d) Review the meaning of Baptism and the teachings of the Church, and also prepare by prayer for the coming event. This can be done either alone or together with the parish priest and other couples whose children are to be baptized at the same time. (Most parishes now provide a program of instruction for parents and godparents; this gives all concerned a solid preparation for intelligent participation in the baptismal ceremony.)

e) Prepare to answer the questions that will be asked during the ceremony and to make the threefold profession of faith during the ceremony.

f) Provide loose garments for the child so that they can be easily removed if Baptism is to be by immersion. The garments should be such that the child can be easily clothed in the baptismal dress at the proper time during the celebration.

g) Encourage the godparents to provide the baptismal dress and candle, and invite them to bring them to the church as their gifts to the child. (A local department store will have a suitable dress for the occasion, and your own church or a religious goods store will have baptismal candles on hand.)

STRUCTURE OF THE CEREMONY

As an aid to better participation in the ceremony it helps to keep the following structure in mind:

Reception of the Children

A fitting hymn may be sung as the celebrant comes to welcome those who are present for the baptismal celebration. He greets all, especially the parents and godparents, and questions them concerning the name of each child and their readiness to assume their parental responsibilities. Then he welcomes the children, signs the cross on the forehead of each and invites the parents (and godparents) to do the same. All then proceed (while singing, if convenient) to where the Liturgy of the Word will take place. (If necessary — and it is convenient to do so — someone, other than the parents and godparents, may take the child or children to another area of the church at this time.)

Celebration of God's Word

One or more of the assigned Scripture passages are read and a homily is given by the priest to explain the sacrament, stir up the faith of all taking part, and encourage the parents to carry out their responsibilities. This may be followed by a period of silence for meditation on what has been read and said. Next come the General Intercessions (Prayers of the Faithful) and a short litany of the saints which may include the patrons of the children to be baptized.

Prayer of Exorcism and Anointing

Next, a prayer asking God to free the child (or children) from the powers of darkness is offered. They are then anointed on the breast with the oil of catechumens, or the celebrant lays his hand on each child in silence.

Celebration of the Sacrament

A fitting hymn may be sung as all proceed to the baptismal font. The celebrant, invoking God and recalling his plan of salvation, blesses the water or commemorates its previous blessing. Turning to the parents, he again stresses their duty to transmit the faith to their offspring. He asks them to make a profession of faith. (See Appendix, page 39.)

If one of the parents cannot make the profession of faith because, for example, he/she is not Catholic, he/she may keep silent. All that is asked of such a one is that permission be given for the child to be instructed in the faith. Obtaining the parents' consent to the Baptism of their child, the celebrant immerses or pours water on each child, saying the customary words.

Then each is anointed with the oil of chrism which signifies the royal priesthood of the baptized and his/her enrollment into the fellowship of God's people. Next, he clothes the child with a white garment which is an outward sign of the child's Christian dignity. Then the child's baptismal candle is lighted from the Easter candle and held by one of the parents or godparents. This is a reminder that the child now enlightened by Christ is to walk always as a child of the light and keep the flame of faith burning throughout life. The "Ephphetha" (prayer over ears and mouth), when it is performed, follows immediately.

Conclusion of the Ceremony

All now go to the altar, again singing a hymn, if feasible. After the priest speaks of the future reception of the Eucharist by the baptized children, everyone prays together the Lord's Prayer, in which God's children pray to their Father in heaven. Finally the priest blesses first the mothers, who hold the children in their arms, then the fathers, and lastly the entire assembly, to ask God's grace in abundance for all. The celebration may conclude with a hymn of thanksgiving or Easter joy, or the "Magnificat."

If Baptism takes place during Sunday Mass, the Mass for the Sunday is used, and the celebration takes place as follows:

At the beginning of Mass the rite of receiving the children takes the place of the greeting and penitential rite.

In the Liturgy of the Word the readings are taken from the Mass of the Sunday (or for special reasons, from those provided in the Baptismal rite); the homily is based on the sacred texts, but should be directed to the Baptism about to take place; the profession of faith takes the place of the creed; and the general intercessions are those used in the Baptismal rite, to which are added the petitions for the universal Church and the needs of the world.

After the prayer of exorcism, anointing and the other baptismal ceremonies, the celebration of Baptism takes place; and the Mass continues in the usual way with the Liturgy of the Eucharist. For the final blessing any one of the formulas provided in the rite for Baptism may be used.

Home Celebration

Since this is an important family occasion, it is fitting that a simple party take place at home after the Baptism. All of those who were invited to the church should be asked to come, including the celebrant of the Baptism, as this will give him an opportunity to become better acquainted with the family.

Older children in the family can be called upon to make decorations and banners. If the family has an Easter candle, it can burn in a place of honor together with the candles received at previous Baptisms. The godparents may be invited to sign the family record book. After the celebration, the candles and white garment should be put away and carefully kept for future use.

III
A PARISH COMMUNITY CELEBRATION

ROLE OF THE PARENTS

Since the parents role in Baptism is a vital and special one, it is imperative that they be present at the celebration in which their child is reborn in water and the Holy Spirit. Along with the assembled community they listen to the words addressed to them and join in the common prayers. They will be called upon to:

a) publicly request that their child be baptized;

b) sign their child with the cross after the priest does so;

c) renounce Satan and make a profession of their faith;

d) carry their child to the font and assist in the Baptism itself (preferably this is done by the mother);

e) accept and hold the lighted candle;

f) receive the blessing for mothers and fathers.

After the Baptism, in gratitude to God and fidelity to the responsibilities they have assumed, they are expected to teach their child by word and example to know and love God, and to see that the child receives Confirmation and takes part in the Eucharist.

ROLE OF THE GODPARENTS

Godparents have been chosen to join in a spiritual way the family of the child to be baptized and to represent the Church at the Baptism. Their presence at the celebration signifies their willingness to help the parents bring up their child to profess and live the faith. They are asked to join the parents in professing the faith in which the child is being baptized.

To fulfill their role, they should be mature enough to assume it, have already received the sacraments of Baptism, Confirmation, and the Eucharist, and be members of the Catholic Church, canonically free to carry out their duties.

However, a baptized and believing Christian may act as a godparent or Christian witness along with a Catholic godparent at the request of the parents and in accord with the directives on this matter issued by the local bishop.

ROLE OF THE PARISH PRIEST

It is the duty of the parish priest, with the help of catechists and other qualified lay people, to prepare parents and godparents with appropriate pastoral guidance, to administer the sacrament, and to help later in the task of Christian formation.

After arrangements for Baptism have been made, the parish priest will, if possible, visit the parents, see that they are visited, or invite them to a meeting, either alone or with a group of other parents, in order to prepare them for the coming celebration by pastoral counsel, instruction, and prayer.

ROLE OF THE PARISH COMMUNITY

Christian instruction and solid preparation for Baptism are of primary concern for the Church. Through the ministry of the Church, infants are baptized and brought up in the faith. The People of God, that is, the Church made present in the local parish community, thus have an important part to play in the Baptism of children. Before and after the celebration of the sacrament, children have a right to the love and help of the community.

In the actual celebration, the People of God (represented not only by the parents, godparents, and relatives but also, as far as possible, by friends, neighbors and some members of the local church) should take an active part, especially when they are called upon to express their assent with the priest after the parents and godparents make the profession of faith. By their active participation in the celebration they show their joy as the newly baptized are received into the community of the Church and indicate that the faith in which the children are baptized is not the private possession of the individual family, but is rather the common treasure of the whole Church of Christ.

So that Baptism may clearly appear as the sacrament of the Church's faith and of admittance into the People of God, it should normally be celebrated in the parish church where there is a font. Baptism should be administered at home only when there is danger of death, and in hospitals only in cases of grave emergency.

To emphasize its paschal character Baptism should, if possible, be celebrated during the Easter Vigil or on Sunday, the day on which the Church commemorates the Lord's Resurrection. Thus, the entire parish community may be present and the necessary relationship between Baptism and the Eucharist can be clearly seen.

When it occurs outside of Mass, Baptism should, whenever possible, be a communal celebration for all the recently born children in the presence of the faithful, or at least of the relatives, friends and neighbors, who are to take an active part in the rite. Baptizing a number of children together is the ideal; for this reason many parishes have designated one Sunday a month as the baptismal day.

Appendix

Since a prominent part of the baptismal ceremony consists of the profession of faith — by parents and godparents — we offer here for your prayful study the questions and answers proposed at that part of the ceremony.

Celebrant: Do you believe in God, the Father Almighty, creator of heaven and earth?
Parents and godparents: I do.

Celebrant: Do you believe in Jesus Christ, his only Son, our Lord, who was born of the Virgin Mary, was crucified, died, and was buried, rose from the dead, and is now seated at the right hand of the Father?
Parents and godparents: I do.

Celebrant: Do you believe in the Holy Spirit, the holy Catholic Church, the communion of saints, the forgive-ness of sins, the resurrection of the body, and life everlasting?
Parents and godparents: I do.

Chapter 3
Confirmation:
Filled With the Spirit

Those who receive the sacrament of Confirmation remember that event for many years to come. Often in later life when happenings of the past become hazy, people can still recall with great clarity the day when they received the fullness of the Holy Spirit in Confirmation. Even though it may have occurred more than a half century earlier, they remember the months of special preparation in religion classes that preceded the great day. Questions and answers had to be memorized. A sponsor had to be chosen. There was constant practice to make sure that the ceremony would proceed smoothly. Finally the day of Confirmation came. The bishop was present, the choir was in full voice, the church was filled with anxious candidates for Confirmation. Well-chosen sponsors, proud parents, relatives, and friends — all waited anxiously for the ceremony to begin.

Each Confirmation is special whether it takes place in the thatch-roofed church of some tropical mission land or in the cathedral church of a large archdiocese anywhere in the world. It is an important day to the people being confirmed, to the members of the local parish, and to the universal Church which increases in holiness each time a member is confirmed in the Holy Spirit. It is hard to imagine that any Confirmation ceremony could be more spectacular or more important than the first Confirmation on Pentecost Sunday when the apostles, along with the Mother of our Lord, were gathered in the upper room. They had spent nine days in prayer as Jesus had directed them. They were waiting for the coming of the Holy Spirit. Then he came.

> Suddenly from up in the sky there came a noise like a strong, driving wind which was heard all through the house where they were seated. Tongues as of fire appeared, which parted and came to rest on each side of them. All were filled with the Holy Spirit . . . (Acts 2:2-4).

Filled with the Spirit they went forth from that room to proclaim the Lord's message to all who had gathered outside.

There is hardly a page in the New Testament or an event in the life of Christ where the presence of the Spirit is not felt and then mentioned in the scriptural account of the occasion. Yet the presence of the Spirit was realized long before this.

HOLY SPIRIT THROUGH THE AGES

In the Old Testament, the action of God is described by the Hebrew word *ruah* which means "breath" or "air." This "breath" is the source of life for all men and for all of creation. It was used to describe God's inner action and influence on the life of men and women everywhere. In Genesis 1:2, God's Spirit stirred up the primeval waters. In Genesis 2:7, that same Spirit breathed life into Adam. The Spirit of the Old Testament was life-giving. It also came to rest on those special people chosen by God to be his spokesmen to the people. The Spirit of God was said to rest on Moses (Nm 11:17). David received the Spirit (1 Sm 16:13) which then spoke through him. God's Spirit spoke through all the prophets as they delivered their message to the people.

The prophets saw that in a future age this Spirit would come upon all people, not just the prophets and leaders of the community.

> Then afterward I will pour out my spirit upon all mankind. Your sons and daughters shall prophesy, your old men shall dream dreams, your young men shall see visions; even upon the servants and the handmaids, in those days, I will pour out my spirit (Jl 3:1-2).

When the prophet first wrote these words, the day of which he spoke was still many generations away. Later, they were fulfilled. Peter was able to quote from this passage on the day of his Confirmation, the first Pentecost.

Those who possess God's Spirit are said to be consecrated, set aside, dedicated to the service of God in some special office or mission. This was to be the case in the life of Jesus. He was prophet. He was the Messiah, the Savior.

Already at his annunciation and birth, the effects of the Holy Spirit were quite evident in his life. Mary and Joseph, Elizabeth, Simeon and Zechariah were all enlightened by the Spirit concerning the plans of God that were coming to pass in the Child named Jesus. The Holy Spirit's intervention was obvious from the moment of the Annunciation when the angel Gabriel proclaimed to Mary, ''. . . The Holy Spirit shall come upon you and the power of the Most High shall overshadow you . . .'' (Lk 1:35). When Jesus began his public ministry, the presence of the Spirit in his life was realized by all. After being baptized by John in the Jordan, the sky opened and the Spirit descended like a dove from the sky to rest on Jesus (Jn 1:33). It was the Spirit who led Jesus from that day forward as he preached and taught all the people, as he healed the sick and restored the dead to life.

At the Last Supper, Jesus proclaimed that the Spirit would enter into a new stage by coming to the apostles and residing in the Church. This Spirit was to be a Spirit of truth proceeding from the Father. It was the Spirit who would bear witness to Christ through the action of the believers. He would come and reside with the Church for all ages, even to the end of time, as soon as Jesus had taken his place at the right hand of the Father. On Easter Sunday, Jesus appeared to the apostles and gave them the power of the Spirit which allowed them to forgive sins and to welcome back those who had strayed (Jn 20:22-23). At the same time the apostles received the command to baptize in the name of the Father, the Son, and the Holy Spirit (Mt 28:19).

This presence of the Holy Spirit in the new Church filled the apostles with the zeal and courage needed by all who are to be public witnesses to Christ, especially in his death and Resurrection. The Spirit also indicated his powerful presence in the early community through many extraordinary gifts. Those possessing the Spirit did great things that led to the conversion of many and the expansion of the Church. Paul wrote to the Corinthians and spoke to them about using properly the many special gifts of the Spirit that they had received. To one the Spirit gave the gift of wisdom in speaking. Another received great faith or the power to heal. Others, again, were able to work miracles through the Spirit. Still others could speak or understand tongues. Prophecy and discernment were the Spirit's gift to others. Regardless of how special these gifts were, they were granted for only one reason. "To each person the manifestation of the Spirit is given for the common good" (1 Cor 12:7).

Today we all celebrate our own Pentecost on the day of our Confirmation. Just as the apostles did on the first Pentecost, Christians, on the day of their Confirmation, become public witnesses to Christ and his work of saving all people. The same Spirit who was foreshadowed in the Old Testament as a "breath" of God, who came in the form of a dove at the Baptism of Jesus, and who came to the apostles in the tongues of fire at Pentecost, now comes to all persons at Confirmation. Divine power is conferred so that all can undertake their Christian commitment seriously and live their faith completely.

Even those already confirmed continue to search for the Spirit in a special way. Here in the U.S. a group called the Catholic Charismatics came into being in early 1967. From a small core of some 90 people they have inflamed the hearts of between one and two million American Catholics. Theirs is a process seen by their leaders not as a movement within the Church, but as a sign of the Church itself being renewed.

Charismatics have, among others, these distinguishing features: they attend prayer meetings on a regular basis, and they emphasize individual charisms (gifts of the Spirit) such as speaking in tongues, prophecy, and the gift of healing. In the forefront of the charismatic renewal is the Holy Spirit, who is regaining the central place he had in the Church described in the Acts of the Apostles. At its deepest level is divine charity, the source of all true charisms.

CONFIRMATION: SACRAMENT OF INITIATION

Confirmation is not our first encounter with the Holy Spirit. That takes place at Baptism. The Trinity comes to dwell in the newly baptized as they are born again in water and the Spirit. Baptism brings people into personal union with God.

They become adopted sons and daughters. Freed from their sins, they become new creations and children of God, able to share in his glory. Should a person die suddenly at a young age or for some serious reason be unable to receive the other sacraments, Baptism is all that is needed for salvation. Thus introduced to the ways of God, the sacraments of Confirmation and the Eucharist continue the process. Baptism initiates a person into the Church; Confirmation completes and perfects Baptism; the Eucharist is the climax of the initiation and the ongoing means toward growth and maturity in faith.

These three sacraments of initiation may be a new idea for many people today. Actually, the concept is as old as the Church. In the year 200, speaking about the sacraments of initiation, it was written:

> The body is washed that the soul may be cleansed;
> the body is overshadowed by the laying on of hands
> that the soul may be enlightened by the Holy Spirit;
> the body is fed on the Body and Blood of Christ
> that the soul too might be nourished by God.

For centuries, whenever people spoke about Confirmation it was in terms of becoming a soldier for Christ. This idea came from the Pentecost sermon given by an otherwise unknown bishop from the southern part of Gaul in the late 500s. Somehow this soldier concept received wide publicity and was used for over a thousand years to explain the main effects of the sacrament of Confirmation. In present times "soldier" is not as popular a term as it once was. To see Confirmation as a sacrament that arms a person for spiritual combat would seem to be in conflict with the many instances where the Spirit brings peace and love to a divided Church which needs to be united by Spirit-filled Christians, not conquered by them.

The documents of the Second Vatican Council dealt with the effects of the sacraments of initiation. They noted that as members of the living Church, all the faithful are made like Christ through Baptism, Confirmation, and Communion. All Christians have the duty of cooperating in the expansion and growth of the Body of Christ. They should foster a truly Catholic spirit, spending their energy to spread the Gospel and lead a Christian life *(see Decree on the Church's Missionary Activity,* 36). By the example of their life and the witness of their speech, Christians should show forth the new man that they put on at Baptism along with the power of the Holy Spirit by whom they were strengthened at Confirmation (see above *Decree,* 11).

In the earliest times Baptism and Confirmation, the first two steps in Christian initiation, were conferred at the same ceremony. Just as the bishop was the lone celebrant of the Mass, so he alone performed all Baptisms and Confirmations. Only when it became physically impossible for the bishop to be present at all Baptisms were adjustments made in the ceremony. The parish priest began to replace the bishop in the sacraments of Baptism and Confirmation as he had already done with the Mass. This is still the case in churches of the Eastern Rite where the priest is the celebrant for Baptism, Confirmation, and Communion. In Rome, however, the final anointing of Baptism and the laying on of hands was done only by a bishop. Thus, Confirmation came to be viewed as a sacrament apart from Baptism. And this practice spread to the rest of Europe in the Middle Ages.

What had begun as a uniform single ceremony of initiation had become three distinct sacraments — Baptism, Confirmation, Communion — each occurring at a different age and stage of Christian development. Baptism was to be for infants. Reception of Communion came when a person reached the age of reason. The sacrament of Confirmation was given at a more advanced age. This was a disruption of the original order of Baptism, Confirmation, and then Communion. Aware of this original format the Second Vatican Council asked that the rite of Confirmation be revised so that the connection between Confirmation and the rest of the process of Christian initiation might be more clearly seen. This is now done by having the renewal of baptismal vows before the actual Confirmation ceremony which then takes place during the Mass so that the newly confirmed can receive Communion.

The revised rite of Confirmation allows episcopal conferences to set the age for this sacrament. In the U.S. some bishops insist that it be administered after the age of reason has been reached and before reception of Communion. This, of course, is theologically correct. However, others — for pastoral reasons — prefer to administer it to adolescents or young adults. These latter bishops see it as an occasion for youth to make a personal choice and adult commitment to their faith received at Baptism. In any case, there is a much stronger emphasis being placed on this sacrament in modern times. The third precept of the Church now reads: "To study Catholic teaching in preparation for the Sacrament of Confirmation, to be confirmed, and then to continue to study and advance the cause of Christ."

MODERN RITE OF CONFIRMATION

Ordinarily Confirmation takes place within the Mass in order to express more clearly the fundamental connection of this sacrament with the entirety of Christian initiation. When Confirmation is conferred within the Mass, the sacramental actions take place after the Liturgy of the Word. The Mass begins in the usual manner with the bishop presiding as the main celebrant assisted by priests as concelebrants. The prayers used during the Mass are a plea for the Spirit to come down among those present to make them temples of glory and witnesses of the Good News to the whole world.

After the Gospel the pastor presents the candidates for Confirmation to the bishop. There is no established custom for this throughout the United States, but if the number to be confirmed is not too great the pastor calls off the name of each candidate. On hearing his/her name each candidate stands in acknowledgment, or comes forward together with his/her sponsor.

After the Gospel and the formal presentation of the candidates, the bishop preaches the homily. Usually he explains the sacrament and relates it to the Biblical readings used during the ceremony. He directs his words to the candidates for Confirmation as well as to the entire assembly. As the successor to the apostles, the bishop has the power to give the Holy Spirit in Confirmation. Although there are no tongues of fire or great winds, the Spirit does come to fill hearts with the love of God to bring people together in one faith, and to work within all people to make the Church one and holy. Those about to be confirmed are encouraged by the bishop to be active members in the Church, alive in Jesus Christ through the guidance of the Holy Spirit. Here he will especially emphasize the gift of fortitude, that moral courage that makes all confirmed become witnesses to Christ, in the Church and before the world.

At the end of the bishop's homily the candidates stand to make a public renewal of their baptismal promises. By this renewal they affirm the pledge that their sponsors made for them at the time of their Baptism. They recall their Baptism and the faith that has been given to them in their youth. Now, speaking for themselves, they pledge to continue in that belief and also to make that faith grow in their own life and throughout the world by the witness that they will give to the Gospel message. The bishop asks several questions to which each candidate responds, "I do." After the questions, the bishop gives his assent to the profession made by the candidates by saying, "This is our faith. This is the faith of the Church. We are proud to profess it in Christ Jesus our Lord." Then all the people respond, "Amen."

The imposition of hands is the next element of the ceremony. Those to be confirmed now kneel, and the bishop asks the people to pray with him for the candidates that God will pour out his Spirit to strengthen them in the faith so that they might be more like Christ, the Son of God. After a time of silent prayer the bishop and all the priests extend their hands over the candidates. The bishop prays that the Father will send the Spirit as helper and guide, bringing to them the spirit of wisdom and understanding, right judgment and courage, knowledge and reverence, together with the spirit of wonder and awe in God's presence. Praying for the coming of the Spirit with outstretched arms can be traced to the New Testament when the apostles confirmed the earliest believers in this way (Acts 8:17).

Next, each candidate, accompanied by his/her sponsor, goes to the bishop. The sponsor places his/her hand on the candidate's shoulder and gives the Confirmation name to the bishop. Each candidate is now anointed on the forehead. The bishop dips his right thumb in the chrism and makes the sign of the cross with the chrism on the candidate's forehead while saying the words, "Be sealed with the Gift of the Holy Spirit."

After the anointing, the bishop gives the sign of peace to the newly confirmed while saying, "Peace be with you." Each candidate responds, "And also with you." The traditional gesture at this moment, the slap on the cheek, no longer takes place. It is to be replaced by the customary sign of peace or friendship. In the United States this is usually a handshake.

The ceremony of Confirmation ends with the Prayer of the Faithful. The bishop asks that the Spirit will make us one. Petitions are made for those just confirmed, for the Church and the whole world, for parents, godparents, and sponsors. The bishop concludes with a prayer asking that the Gospel will be spread far and wide by those who have just received the Spirit.

After the ceremony of Confirmation, the Liturgy of the Eucharist is celebrated in the usual manner. Some of the newly confirmed may bring the gifts to the altar. Communion may be distributed under both the forms of bread and wine. In place of the simple blessing at the end of Mass, the bishop may choose a longer form of the final blessing and dismissal. This blessing prayer recalls what has happened at this special ceremony.

PREPARATION FOR CONFIRMATION

The ceremony of Confirmation, when it occurs during the Mass, usually takes less than two hours even with a large group of candidates and much singing. The spiritual effect generated by the sacrament lasts a lifetime. But before there can be a ceremony of Confirmation there has to be a period of preparation. Most of this centers on the person who will receive the sacrament.

Confirmation classes are held for those who attend the parochial school, and special classes are conducted for those in parish programs of religious education. This period of instruction may last a full school year or even longer in some cases. It begins with review of the basic teachings of the faith. It also looks at the meaning of this sacrament in the student's life. The candidate studies the effects of the Spirit upon God's chosen people throughout the Old and New Testaments. Special emphasis is placed upon the Spirit's presence in the life of Christ and then in the Church. Then the ceremony of Confirmation and its various parts are studied so that the candidate understands thoroughly the full meaning of the sacrament. Also, Baptism and the Eucharist, the other two sacraments of initiation, are reexamined in the light of Confirmation.

The minimum age for Confirmation is seven years, but in the United States it is the established practice to delay this sacrament until the child has begun to grow and show signs of maturity. This often means that Confirmation takes place sometime between the sixth and eighth grade in school. Since it is customary at this age to give children more responsibility at home, this is now extended to the parish setting. Many parishes stress the fact that Confirmation makes a person a witness to Christ. This is done through a program where the candidates spend a specific number of hours in service for the parish and its members. It can involve raking leaves or mowing lawns around the church, visiting a shut-in member of the parish, even tutoring a younger student in a special religion class. To further determine the candidate's maturity, many pastors have each child write him a short letter explaining why he wants to be confirmed. It might also be arranged for the candidate to meet with the pastor or one of his assistants for a brief interview and review shortly before the time of Confirmation.

It is the pastor's responsibility to see that candidates for Confirmation are properly instructed, know what they are doing when they renew their baptismal promises, and fittingly prepare their souls to receive this new sacrament. It is especially the responsibility of Christian parents to see that their children are strengthened in the truths of the faith and initiated into the sacramental life of the Church. The entire parish has a responsibility to the person being confirmed.

Sponsors also have essential roles in the celebration of this sacrament. Having one sponsor for the entire group of children is no longer the practice. Individual sponsors present their candidates to the bishop for anointing. Sponsors assume the task of helping the candidates to fulfill their baptismal promises faithfully under this deeper influence of the Holy Spirit. Because of the close connection between each of the three sacraments of initiation it is desirable that one of the godparents from Baptism also be the sponsor at Confirmation.

Choice of a special sponsor for Confirmation is allowed. It is also permissible for parents to be the sponsors for their children at Confirmation. It is no longer necessary that the sponsor be the same sex as the candidate. Pastors should make sure that sponsors are spiritually qualified for their roles. This includes a proper degree of maturity on the part of the sponsor, who must also be a member of the Catholic Church and have already received the three sacraments of initiation: Baptism, Confirmation, and Communion.

WHAT CONFIRMATION DOES

The reception of the Holy Spirit at Confirmation denotes first of all the official perfection and completion of Baptism. It also produces a deepening of our friendship with God, a more personal union with the Spirit of Christ, a pledge of God's commitment to us, the strength to persevere as a good member of God's family, and finally a promise of eternal happiness. Confirmation should deepen our Christian life. We should encounter Christ at a level of greater maturity. The imprint of the Spirit should bring us closer to the image of God. This should then lead us to realize more fully our calling to be witnesses for Christ by the life that we live and the message that we proclaim.

It should be obvious that the coming of the Spirit is not a magical event. It will still be difficult to live in peace and harmony with the people around us and with the members of our family. Life's problems will still come our way. It will still be a struggle to turn the other cheek, to do the Christian thing, to build up the Body of Christ rather than tear it down. But we have the Spirit within us; all we have to do is call when we are in need. With his coming to us in Confirmation we have a special claim to his assistance. And what does the Spirit bring? Throughout the ages, the Church has spoken of the seven special gifts of the Spirit that are received in Confirmation:

> The Spirit of the Lord shall rest upon him;
> a spirit of wisdom and understanding,
> a spirit of counsel and of fortitude,
> a spirit of knowledge, piety, and
> fear of the Lord (Is 11:2-3).

These gifts of the Spirit were present in the early Church (read chapter 2 of Acts). They are also present today in the same magnificent way, provided we use them properly for the building up of the Church. Catholic charismatic renewal — when based on Sacred Scripture as the Good News, Christianity as the outpouring of God's love, and charity as a total way of life — seems to be clear evidence of that.

HOW TO USE THE SPIRIT'S GIFTS

The main purpose of these gifts is to live the life of the beatitudes. Read them in Matthew 5:3-10 and think about them. Apply them to your present situation. Look at the people you live with. Examine your spiritual state of life.

What we must do is to take the first part of each beatitude and live it in our daily life. We must be meek and poor in spirit. A spirit of peace and a clean heart must guide our life. We must search for justice and then be willing to show mercy, realizing that suffering and mourning will be our part as we work for justice. In all these efforts Christ must be our model and guide.

The beatitudes have to be practiced every day if we are to become holy and reach happiness. It isn't enough to act solely with our human talents. We need that Spirit of Confirmation working within us if we are to see clearly the Christian vision. Struggling and suffering are part of the Christian way to happiness. This is not a popular teaching yet it is the way shown to us by Christ, especially in his death on the Cross. If we try to live this life, the Spirit will prompt us to serve all people and to see that justice is done. We will be inspired to take a personal part in spreading Christ's message to everyone. Service of others in the Church should be the characteristic mark of the person who has been confirmed and is now trying to extend the presence of the Holy Spirit in daily life. We must remember that Christ said, "I did not come to be served, but to serve." We too are God's servants when we follow his will for us. That will calls us to do many particular things in our life, but those things always pertain to the building up of the kingdom of God on earth.

Just as there are great demands placed on those who have been confirmed, there are great rewards for those who answer the call. The second part of each beatitude lists those rewards that await us. We shall possess the earth, satisfied and comforted. Better than that, we shall be called children of God, heaven shall be our possession, and we shall see God face-to-face forever. All this can be ours if we realize that the Spirit is present within us ready to use his special gifts to help us live out our Christian life of service. All we have to do is ask.

Come, Holy Spirit,
fill the hearts of your faithful,
enkindle in them the fire of your love.
Send forth your Spirit
and you shall renew the face of the earth.

Chapter 4
Eucharist:
Center of Christian Life

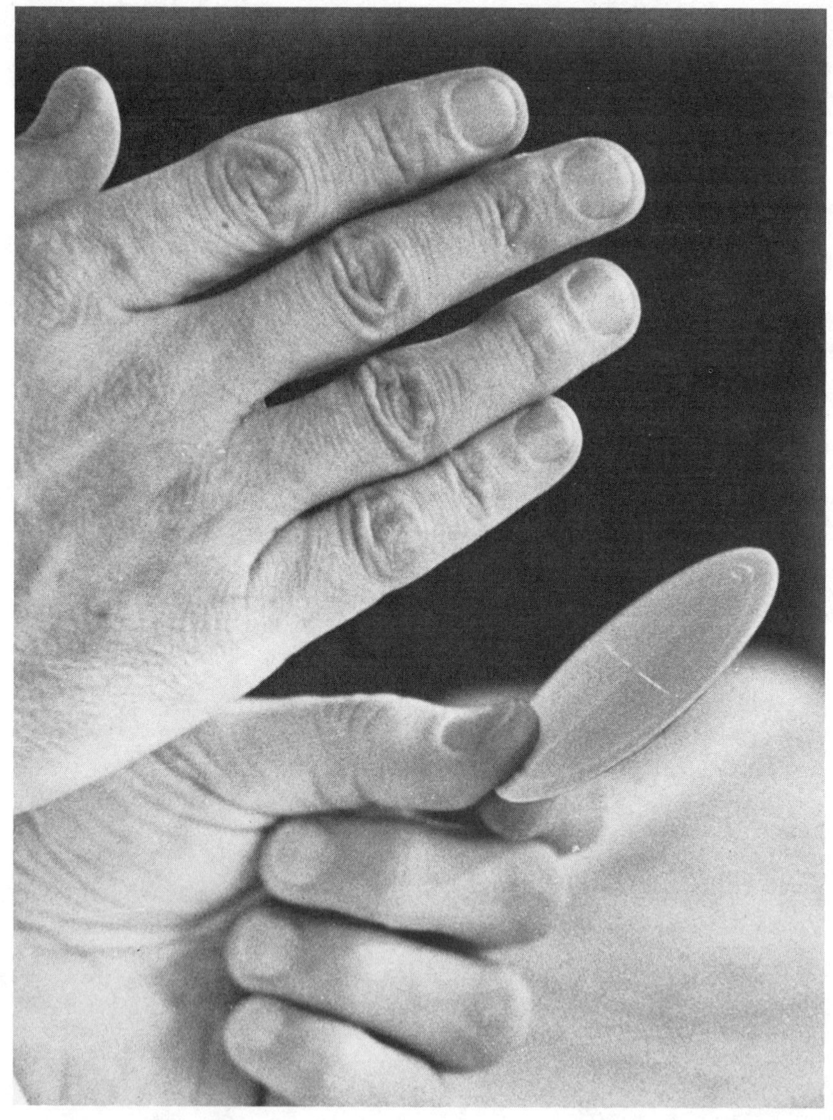

The purpose of these pages is to explain clearly the signs by which the Eucharist is celebrated as the memorial of the Lord and worshiped as a permanent sacrament in the Church. For, although this sacrament is unique in the sense that it makes Christ, the author of holiness, present to us, it is a symbol of a sacred reality and the visible form of an invisible grace — which is one way to define a sacrament. Consequently, the better we understand the signs by which it is celebrated and worshiped, the better will be our participation in the Eucharist.

In the past we tended to divide the Eucharist into three separate parts: the Real Presence, the Sacrifice of the Mass (Eucharist as sacrifice), and Communion (Eucharist as sacrament). Because of this, Communion was not always seen as participation in the Mass, and devotion to the Real Presence was separated from the Sacrifice and from Communion.

Here we wish to explain the Eucharist as the mystery of our faith (Real Presence, true sacrifice, sign of the coming kingdom), the sacramental Sacrifice of the Mass (which memorializes Christ's death and Resurrection), and the worship of the Eucharist as a permanent sacrament. The sacrament of the Eucharist is an action which took place centuries ago and at the same time an action which we perform daily in our lives. The questions we must answer are these: "What did Jesus and his disciples do at the Last Supper? What was the meaning of what they did?" and "What are we doing at the Eucharist? What do we mean by what we are doing?"

I
MYSTERY OF OUR FAITH

Standing at the true center of the sacred liturgy and indeed of our whole Christian life, the Eucharist is rightly called the mystery of faith. It is named "Eucharist," or thanksgiving, either because at its institution Christ "gave thanks," or because it is the supreme act of Christian gratitude to God. The documents of Vatican II and other statements from Roman pontiffs have emphasized the importance of this mystery. Our prayerful understanding of it will be reflected in our lives.

"In the human nature united to himself, the Son of God, by overcoming death through his own death and resurrection, redeemed man and changed him into a new creation (see Gal 6:15; 2 Cor 5:17). For by communicating his Spirit, Christ mystically constitutes as his body those brothers of his who are called together from every nation. In that body the life of Christ is communicated to those who believe and who, through the sacraments, are united in a hidden and real way to Christ in his passion and glorification" *(Const. on the Church, 7).*

"At the Last Supper, on the night he was betrayed, our Savior instituted the eucharistic sacrifice of his Body and Blood. This he did in order to perpetuate the sacrifice of the Cross throughout the ages until he should come again, and so to entrust to his beloved Spouse, the Church, a memorial of his death and resurrection: a sacrament of love, a sign of unity, a bond of charity, a paschal banquet in which Christ is consumed, the mind is filled with grace, and a pledge of future glory is given to us" *(Const. on the Liturgy, 47).*

Therefore, the Mass, the Lord's Supper, is at the same time and inseparably:

A *sacrifice* in which the sacrifice of the cross is perpetuated;

A *memorial* of the death and Resurrection of the Lord;

A *sacred banquet* at which the People of God consume the body and blood of Christ, share in the benefits of the Paschal Sacrifice, renew the New Covenant which God made for all through the blood of Christ, and receive a pledge of future glory in God's kingdom.

In the Mass, therefore, the sacrifice and sacred meal belong to the same mystery. For in it our Lord is immolated when, as Paul VI in his *Mystery of Faith* says, "he begins to be present sacramentally as the spiritual food of the faithful under the appearance of bread and wine." Thus, participation in the Lord's Supper is always Communion with Christ offering himself for us as a sacrifice to the Father.

The Eucharist is the true center of the whole Christian life both for the universal Church and for her local congregations. The other sacraments, every ministry of the Church, each apostolic work — all are linked with the Eucharist and are directed toward it. For it contains the entire spiritual good of the Church, namely, Christ himself.

"It is the summit of both the action by which God sanctifies the world in Christ, and the worship which men offer to Christ and which through him they offer to the Father in the Spirit" (*Const. on the Liturgy,* 10). Through it we express in our lives and manifest to others the mystery of Christ and the true nature of the Church.

By means of the Eucharist the Church continually lives and grows. Every gathering around the altar under the sacred ministry of the bishop, or a priest who takes his place, is a sign of that charity and unity of the Mystical Body, without which there can be no salvation. Truly, the Eucharist, celebrated according to the Lord's will, signifies and effects the unity of all who believe in him.

REAL PRESENCE

Because it efficaciously reproduces the Last Supper, the Eucharist gives us the Real Presence of Christ as our food and drink. It is a true sacrifice, the memorial of Christ's Passion. It is the proclamation of his return: "Each time that you eat this bread and drink this cup, you proclaim the death of the Lord until he comes" (1 Cor 11:26).

Christ is present to us in many ways. He is always present in his Church, especially in her liturgical celebrations. He is present in the Eucharistic sacrifice not only in the person of his minister but especially in the bread and wine changed into his body and blood. By his power he is present in the sacraments; when someone baptizes another it is Christ himself who baptizes. He is present in his Word, since it is he himself who speaks when the Holy Scriptures are read. And he is present when the Church prays and sings, for he has promised "where two or three are gathered together in my name there am I in the midst of them" (Mt 18:20).

The Real Presence is a mystery which we accept on the words of Christ himself, "This is my Body . . . this is my

Blood," and which we affirm when we answer "Amen" to the words "The Body of Christ" spoken by the minister of Communion.

The four accounts of the Last Supper (1 Cor 11:23-25; Lk 22:13-20; Mk 14:16-25; Mt 26:19-29) all agree on essentials. They also point out the paschal character of the Last Supper which prescribed the eating of the lamb — a further reminder that our faith in the Real Presence can be fully developed in relation to sacrifice and Communion.

The Church has always taken literally Christ's words at the Last Supper repeated in the celebration of the Eucharist. Before the consecration there were bread and wine; after the words of consecration there are the body and blood of Christ. This change has come to be called "transubstantiation." The substance of what still looks and tastes like bread and wine has now been changed into the substance of the body and blood of Christ. This constitutes Christ's sacramental presence in contrast to his natural presence.

TRUE SACRIFICE

That the Church is offering a sacrifice to God in the Mass is clearly indicated by the words she uses in its celebration. (See the first Eucharistic Prayer, for example.) The Mass is a sacrifice because in it Christ is offered as a Victim. As the only Victim pleasing to God, he offered his sacrifice once for all on the Cross. In the Mass, however, he offers himself (through the ministry of priests) in a different manner. This manner, or mode, is sacramental; he offers himself in unbloody immolation through the ritual of the Eucharist. So, the Mass is an effective memorial of the sacrifice of the Cross. But to understand how it is a sacrifice and our sacrifice we must first see the death of Christ as a sacrifice and then the connection between the sacrifice of the Cross and the Last Supper, reproduced in the sacramental sacrifice of the Eucharist.

To do this we must examine the Biblical figures and the development of the idea of sacrifice in the Old Testament. Abel, Abraham, and Melchizedek show us how sacrifice developed. (Read Gn 4:2-5; Gn 14:17-20; Ps 109:4.) The deliverance of the Hebrews from Egypt and their journey to the Promised Land were begun with sacrifice. Each family was to slay a lamb, then take the blood and put it on the two doorposts and the entrance to their house. The Lord would spare the houses thus marked when he passed by to strike the land of Egypt (Ex 12:1-7, 12-13).

This sacrifice was to lead up to a family meal at which the lamb was to be completely eaten. As soon as they left the table they went out into the night toward the Red Sea and the Promised Land (Ex 12:7-11). And each year they were to commemorate this sacrifice and meal.

These and other imperfect sacrifices mentioned throughout the Old Testament were climaxed by the prophecy of Malachi: "For from the rising of the sun, even to its setting, my name is great among the nations; and everywhere they bring sacrifice to my name, and a pure offering" (1:11).

The death of Christ on the Cross fulfilled all the prophecies and realized all the figures drawn in the Old Testament. The offering of Christ on the Cross is the true sacrifice of the New Law, the perfect and efficacious sacrifice. This is clearly affirmed in the New Testament, especially in Acts 8:32-33, in John 1:29, and in 1 Corinthians 5:7.

If, then, Christ died once for all in expiation for all sins (see Hebrews 7:27; 9:12, 26-28), how can we take part in that sacrifice and how can we offer Christ so that he will be our sacrifice? This is possible because Christ inaugurated his Pasch by the Last Supper. He encompassed the whole of the next day's sacrifice in a sign, and provided for the renewal of this sign.

Last Supper: Sign of Christ's Sacrifice

We understand the Eucharist better when we examine its signs (bread and wine) and the words which Christ spoke at its institution. The Last Supper is the beginning of the Passion. One flows into the other. Christ's death on the Cross was the immolation of the Paschal Lamb. The Last Supper was the paschal meal in which the Paschal Lamb was eaten. From this meal Christ and his disciples went out into the night for the New Exodus. While in the figurative

Pasch the immolation preceded this meal, here the meal precedes the immolation.

That bread is a sign of Christ's Passion is indicated especially in the Gospel of John. The bread he promised is his flesh to be given "for the salvation of the world" (6:51). Wine is the drink of the covenant between God and man. This theme of the Last Supper is expressed in several of Christ's parables and particularly by the miracle at Cana. But these Biblical indications can be properly understood only in the light of Christ's own words at the Last Supper.

The words of Christ gathered together at consecration time in the liturgy clearly signify his Passion. "This is my body which will be given up for you." "This is the cup of my blood, the blood of the new and everlasting covenant. It will be shed for you and for all men so that sins may be forgiven."

This "new and everlasting covenant" is the one referred to by Jeremiah (31:31-34). Christ at the Last Supper celebrated the liturgy of the New Covenant, already presenting his blood outpoured. He clearly effected a sacramental identity between the Eucharist and his death on the Cross. He committed himself, freely gave himself up to his coming death, already sacramentally present and anticipated in his Eucharist.

That Christ intended the Last Supper to be renewed is evident from his words: "Do this in memory of me." His apostles responded with "the breaking of bread" wherever they went in their missionary travels. And the Church today offers this same true sacrifice.

SIGN OF THE COMING KINGDOM

According to St. Paul (1 Cor 11:26) in the renewal of the Last Supper we "proclaim the death of the Lord, *until he comes.*" We recall this fact at Mass in our Memorial Acclamations, for example: Christ has died, Christ is risen, Christ will come again. The Christ who suffered is present, but the Christ who is present can no longer suffer. He is present in glory.

The Eucharist contains the whole Pasch of Christ, his passage from this world to his Father. And this is emphasized especially by the meal aspect of the Mass. Although the sacrifice is completed with the words of consecration, the Eucharist is meant to be completed in a meal. For, besides bringing personal grace to each communicant, Communion is a sign of the Church and the anticipation of the heavenly banquet.

The Church will be completely whole only when charity is perfect and her union with God no longer needs any intermediary. Consequently, the Eucharist as a mystery of faith is the announcement of and the preparation for the return of Christ and the Kingdom to come.

II

SACRAMENTAL SACRIFICE OF THE MASS

In the foregoing pages we answered the questions: "What did Jesus and his disciples do at the Last Supper and what was the meaning of what they did?" Here we wish to answer the questions: "What are we doing at the Eucharist and what do we mean by what we are doing?"

Before we begin it is well to note that the Roman (or Western) rite is not the only legitimate rite. Egypt, Constantinople, Armenia, the West Syrians and East Syrians all have their own liturgies dating back to ancient times. The Eastern liturgy (Eucharistic celebration) is essentially the same as the Roman Mass, although there are accidental differences, of course.

Having already discussed the Eucharist as the mystery of faith, we now look at it as a sacramental sacrifice — what we describe in popular terms as the Mass.

Ours is the liturgical generation. The aspect of the Eucharist that is being emphasized today is the Mass. To achieve the desired emphasis on the Mass and to avoid a possible "conflict of interest," the tabernacle has been removed from the altar of sacrifice and has been placed in some other part of the sanctuary or in a separate chapel reserved for that purpose. This does not mean, as some people seem to think, that the Blessed Sacrament is being downgraded in any way or that our Lord is not really present there. Emphasis placed on one aspect of the Eucharist does not deny or exclude its other aspects.

Private and Public Prayer

The liturgy is really the official public prayer of the Church. It is distinguished from the private prayer of the individual. Some seem to think that the distinction is between liturgical prayer and personal prayer. To such people the liturgy is a threat to personal piety and true devotion. But nothing could be further from the truth. All prayer, if it is genuine, is personal. Liturgical prayer is the public expression of interior faith, hope, and love, or it is nothing. Celebrating Mass is preeminently an act of faith.

Both private and liturgical prayer are of course necessary and essential. In fact, we cannot really celebrate the liturgy without having prepared ourselves beforehand with private prayer. And then it is private prayer which prolongs and brings to fruition the great graces of the liturgy.

The distinction between private prayer and the liturgy can be illustrated by the example of a United States senator. A senator performs many acts as a private individual. For example, he may read the Declaration of Independence and the Constitution of the United States. Less often he participates in an official act of Congress. When Congress is in session and he is voting on a bill, he is officially and most specifically acting as a senator.

Now it will be well for a senator to read these important documents, the Declaration and Constitution, many times. But the time and the place for him to do so is not when Congress is in session and is voting on a bill. Then he should be participating in this official act of Congress. This is what he was elected for!

In a similar way we as Christians say many private prayers as individual persons: morning and evening prayers; grace at meals; the rosary; the stations of the cross; and perhaps other favorite prayers. Less often we participate in the official public prayers of the Church — the liturgy. In so doing, we are acting most officially and specifically as Christians.

As Christians we should say these private prayers often, even daily, but the time and the place to say them is not when the People of God have gathered together to celebrate the liturgy. We should be participating in this official act of worship of the Church. This is what we were baptized for!

Here, of course, we all must learn to be tolerant. Older people have grown to love the liturgy of their youth. We must remember that for these people it is not just a question of changing some externals of the Mass. The old Latin liturgy was intimately associated with and woven into all of the crucial events of a long lifetime. It held for them memories of birth, marriage, death, and all of the critical moments in-between — each one heavily laden with deep emotional overtones. Now it is as though a great part of their life has suddenly been taken away, since they are not able to identify these past events with the new liturgy.

Worship Not Changeless

It would be strange indeed if the living worship of a living people were changeless. Yet that is the impression many people have. They think that throughout history the Mass has remained changeless. Of course, the history they are thinking of is the 50 or so year-span of their own lifetime. It is true that, until Vatican II, the liturgy has changed very little during our lifetime. In fact, it has not changed much at all since about 1570, shortly after the Council of Trent.

But the full history of the Church reveals that the Mass has been anything but changeless. For example, the language our Lord used in his first Mass at the Last Supper was Aramaic. Then in the following three centuries the Mass was said in Greek. In the 17th century, Jesuit missionaries to China asked for and received from the Holy See permission to celebrate all of the liturgy in Chinese.

The rubrics, which regulate the manner of saying Mass, are another good example of change. One of the characteristics of the Mass, as we knew it before the Council, was the almost complete uniformity in the manner of celebrating it.

But it was not always thus. These rubrics were instituted by the Congregation of Rites which came into existence in the 16th century. Prior to that time there was only basic conformity to what our Lord did at the Last Supper; the *manner* in which this was done was left to the discretion of the celebrant. Now the *Constitution on the Liturgy* permits many legitimate options in the manner of celebrating Mass.

Total Priesthood of Christ

One of the reasons for the recent changes in the liturgy is the renewed emphasis that Vatican II has placed on the total priesthood of Christ. It has always been Catholic doctrine that this priesthood embraces three sacraments.

The sacrament of Baptism in which we receive an indelible character marking us as Christians gives us a participation in the priesthood of Christ.

The sacrament of Confirmation in which we receive a second indelible character gives us a greater participation in the priesthood of Christ.

The sacrament of Holy Orders in which we receive a third indelible character gives priests the power to change bread and wine into the body and blood of Christ and to forgive sins.

This was the teaching of the Church from the beginning. "But you are a chosen race, a royal priesthood, a consecrated nation, a people set apart to sing the praises of God who called you out of darkness into his wonderful light" (1 Pt 2:9).

Though the ministerial priesthood and the priesthood of the faithful differ essentially, they are nonetheless ordered one to another; each in its own proper way shares in the one priesthood of Christ. At Mass the ministerial priest in the person of Christ effects the Eucharistic sacrifice and offers it to God in the name of all the people. The faithful, by virtue of their royal priesthood, participate in the offering of the Eucharist (see *Const. on the Church,* 10).

The changes in the new liturgy are demanded by this new emphasis on the priesthood of the faithful. All those who are baptized, and much more so those who are also confirmed, are members of the priesthood of Christ and actually offer up the sacrifice of the Mass together with the ministerial priest who has received Holy Orders. Therefore the altar must be turned around and brought out to them. If they are to participate, the liturgy must be in their language. They must have their own specified parts to perform. They may be commentators, lectors, and bearers of the gifts in the offertory procession. And all members of the congregation, not just a group of professionals, are asked to do the singing. All the People of God, together with the ministerial priest, are to be actively drawn into the sacrifice because they truly offer their lives with Christ to the Father.

RITE OF THE MASS

Now that we have become familiar with the new rite of the Mass we can see clearly how the Liturgy of the Word and the Liturgy of the Eucharist constitute a single act of worship. When we hear the Word of God we realize that the wonders it proclaims culminate in the paschal mystery, of which the memorial is sacramentally celebrated in the Mass. Thus, we are nourished by the bread of life which we find at the table both of the Word of God and of the Body of Christ.

Liturgy of the Word

After the introductory rites which consist of a greeting, a penitential ceremony, a hymn of praise (the Gloria), and an opening prayer, we listen to and respond to the Word of God. On Sundays, for example, the three readings will be from the Old Testament, the Epistles (usually), and from the Gospels. These are followed by a homily, the profession of faith (Creed), and the prayers of the faithful. All this is not meant simply to teach or edify. More than that, the Word of God is considered as a special presence of Christ, its proclamation an authentic way of reliving his mysteries.

Like the disciples on the road to Emmaus (Lk 24:13-32), we prepare for the Eucharist by listening to the Word of God. The various readings of the sacred texts cause us to enter successively into the various aspects of Christ's mysteries in the course of the liturgical year. The Eucharist would be unintelligible without the Gospel. And without the Eucharist the Christ of the Gospel would remain distant: his Word only becomes clear when we take part in offering his sacrifice and experiencing his presence and friendship in Communion.

Liturgy of the Eucharist

This part of the Mass simply reproduces and develops the actions and words of Christ at the Last Supper. There he took bread, and having given thanks, he broke it and gave it to them, saying: "This is my Body." Then, taking the cup, he gave thanks and gave it to them saying: "This is my Blood." These are the integral parts of the sacrifice of the Mass: offertory (the offering of bread and wine), consecration (the changing of the bread and wine into the body and blood of Christ). When we have these three elements properly actualized we have the sacrifice of Calvary offered up now in an unbloody manner, infinitely pleasing to the Father. And this happens through the action of Christ, regardless of the sanctity or lack of it on the part of the celebrant.

The four Eucharistic Prayers begin with introductory dialogue to the preface which is followed by the first acclamation of the people (Holy, holy, holy Lord). After the celebrant prays the words of consecration, all proclaim the mystery of faith — Christ now truly, really, and substantially present on the altar.

Communion Rite

The supreme prayer of preparation for Communion is the Our Father. After the celebrant has consumed the body and blood of Christ, he distributes Communion to the faithful. Communion is received on the tongue, or it may also be received in the hand if the bishop of the local diocese has granted this permission. One who receives in this way should accept the Host in his or her cupped hand, step to one side, pick up the Host with the other hand, and immediately consume it.

Besides the grace flowing from the offering of the sacrifice (which is why we ask priests to offer Mass for special intentions), there are special graces connected with sacramental participation through Communion. By its nature Communion is a sacrificial meal at which we partake of the offering that has been accepted by God and so enter intimately into his life.

On this account the Church prescribes "that no one conscious of mortal sin, even though he/she seems to be contrite, may go to the Holy Eucharist without previous sacramental confession." In urgent necessity and if no confessor is available, he/she should simply make an act of perfect contrition with the intention of confession individually, at the proper time, the mortal sins which he/she cannot confess at present.

Positive conditions for receiving Communion are the right intention (not out of routine or human respect, but for the purpose of pleasing God) and observance of the Communion fast. This fast means that we may not eat anything or drink anything (other than water) one hour before the reception of Communion. The sick and the aged need fast for only 15 minutes and they may take nonalcoholic beverages and liquid or solid medicines without any time limit.

When we receive Communion worthily the graces received are in the first place personal. "He who eats my flesh and drinks my blood lives on in me and I in him" (Jn 6:56). But the Eucharist is also a sign of unity, since we receive it from the Church at a family meal in which all partake of the same bread. Perhaps we have over-emphasized the personal aspect in the past; and in doing so we have neglected the social aspect — our union with one another through Christ.

The Eucharist is the summit and source of all holiness. But real holiness consists in the love of our neighbor as well as the love of God. Formerly, some may have restricted their attention to the vertical — the love of God. Now the pendulum has swung to the opposite extreme and many seem to be exclusively concerned with the horizontal — the love of neighbor. They tell us that "Christ is the man for others." But they forget that he also came to do the will of his Father and spent whole nights in prayer.

Both of these loves are necessary; we cannot have one without the other. "If anyone says that he loves God whom he does not see and does not love his neighbor whom he does see, he is a liar" (1 Jn 4:20). The converse is equally true. Maybe we can love those who love us without a great love of God, but it is impossible to love those whom we find naturally repugnant — especially those whom we consider to be our enemies — without a great love of God.

A Christianity restricted to either one of these two loves would be easy. But to keep them both requires great courage. When we balance the vertical with the horizontal we form a cross. And that is the crux of the matter. Real Christian love demands courage. If we despise one of the two arms of Christian love, we climb down from the cross.

Communion helps us to acquire this love of our neighbor. It gives us the grace necessary for this universal love. In uniting us to Christ it also unites us to everyone else who is united to him. In Christ we are all one, one family, one People of God. "No Christian community can be built up unless it has its basis and center in the celebration of the most Holy Eucharist. Here, therefore, all education in the spirit of community must originate" *(Decree on the Life and Ministry of Priests,* 6).

LAST SUPPER, CRUCIFIXION, MASS

Truly, then, the Mass is a sacramental sacrifice. It is a memorial of our Lord's death and Resurrection. The sacrifice of the Cross is the sacrifice of the Church which she makes present in all times and in all places. It is a true sacrifice, enabling all Christians to adore and praise God by, with, and through Christ, our High Priest. Because this sacrifice is sacramental, it is not something added to the sacrifice of Calvary. Christ's death on the Cross remains always unique, accomplished once for all. The memorial of his death — as depicted in the Last Supper — is repeated in Masses throughout the world.

As the Last Supper was a sacramental sacrifice, so the Mass is a sacramental sacrifice because Christ celebrates it through the minister who acts in his person. The separate consecration of bread and wine is a sign of the sacrifice. In the Passion of Christ, his blood was separated from his body. This is symbolized by the separate consecration of bread and wine in the Mass.

This offering of Christ by the Church is sacramental; she does it through signs. Christ offers himself through the priest who consecrates; he in turn represents the Church because he takes the role of Christ, the head of his Mystical Body. A consecrating priest is therefore necessary. The faithful unite themselves with him — by giving thanks, making remembrance of the Passion of Christ, and offering the immaculate Victim. This active internal participation is expressed externally by their words, silence, song, and posture.

III
PERMANENT SACRAMENT

The original reason for reservation of the Eucharist in our churches was for the administration of Viaticum — Communion to the dying. (Facing the last stage in our journey to God, we find strength and security in the Eucharist, the pledge of eternal happiness.) It was also reserved so that Communion could be brought to the sick, and so that people could adore our Lord, Jesus Christ present in the sacrament.

Special devotion to our Lord in the Blessed Sacrament grew gradually in the Church — and for many reasons. One powerful influence was the fact that the faithful saw the Lord only briefly (at the Elevation) and when they received him personally — which in certain ages was not too often. In fact, it was because of this last fact that the Church had to prescribe under pain of sin the reception of Communion at least once a year at Easter time.

The *Constitution on the Liturgy* placed special emphasis on the celebration of the Eucharist. The Mass is the center of Christian life. The Eucharist contains the entire spiritual treasure of the Church, Christ himself, our Passover and living bread. This emphasis, however, was not meant to downgrade such devotional practices as Benediction and personal visits to the Blessed Sacrament. Personal, private faith in the Real Presence of the Lord leads naturally to external, public expression of this faith.

What the Church desires is that these services take into account the liturgical seasons, that they harmonize with the sacred liturgy in some sense, by taking their origin from it and by leading us back to it. And this is done when we remember that Christ's presence in our midst is derived from the sacrifice. His principal desire in instituting the Eucharist is to be with us as food, medicine, and comfort.

When our piety moves us to adore the Blessed Sacrament we are inspired to participate more fully in the paschal mystery (the Passion, death, and Resurrection of Christ). By remaining closely united to Christ, we enjoy intimate familiarity with him and offer heartfelt prayer to him for ourselves, for all those who are dear to us, for peace and for salvation of the world. And thus we offer our entire lives with Christ to the Father in the Holy Spirit. In this way, too, we develop the right dispositions for devoutly celebrating the memorial of the Lord and for receiving frequently the heavenly bread which the Father has provided for us.

Conclusion

It is hoped that these pages have clarified the reader's understanding of the Eucharist. What is important to remember is that this "mystery of faith" is based on the paschal mystery which enables us to understand the unity that exists between the Last Supper, the sacrifice of the Cross, and the sacramental sacrifice of the Mass. It is at once the memorial of Christ's saving death, the presence among us today of the risen Christ, and the anticipation and pledge of his return. It is a sacrifice and a banquet, an intimate meeting with the Lord and a supremely communal action. All these interwoven aspects are those of the paschal mystery. By following God's education of his people through the Old Testament we reach a rightful understanding of the realities of the New.

Recent changes in the liturgy of the Mass have tried to emphasize this point. However, the changes themselves have not made everyone happy. Some are disturbed because there are points of difference in the various dioceses — about Saturday evening Masses, about wedding Mass times, etc. But this is an exercise in collegiality. The Holy See gives a certain permission to the universal Church; the individual bishop determines whether or not the permission will be allowed in his diocese. The *Constitution on the Liturgy* advises bishops: "The age and condition of their people, their way of life and degree of religious culture should be taken into account" (19).

Perhaps some people are expecting too much from these changes which are mostly external. What is needed is interior change. As the Scripture says, "Change not your garments, change your heart." There is danger that our worship of God could become wholly external and merit Christ's condemnation (quoting Isaiah) of the Pharisees: "This people pays me lip service, but their heart is far from me" (Mt 15:8).

Our hearts will be in our liturgy when the Eucharistic mystery is understood and lived as described here. Why? Because the Eucharist gives us the insight that reconciles the apparent paradoxes in God's plan for our salvation. The celebration of the Eucharist is the supreme act of unselfish love, directed to God in adoration and thanksgiving. At the same time it is atonement for our sins, and intercession for all our needs. It is at once the gift of God to man and man's supreme response to God in Christ. At one and the same time, it gives glory to God and brings sanctity to men in Christ.

SACRAMENTS OF RENEWAL

Penance (Reconciliation):
Called Back to the Father's Love

Anointing of the Sick:
Strength for Soul, Mind, and Body

The sacraments of initiation which we have just treated give us a good start in our following of Christ. As children of God, we mature in the Spirit and are constantly nourished by the Bread of Life.

Despite this, however, in our human weakness we fall into sin. With our God-given free wills, we choose evil instead of good. The idea of sin, then, is the reverse side of the idea of God. Only the discovery of God makes possible a true discovery of sin. Sin certainly causes shame, suffering and death (see Gn 3), but essentially it is a willful abandonment of God. More than an act of disobedience, it is a sign of unfaithfulness in our love for him. This is why we must admit our sins not only to ourselves but primarily to God.

It would be sad indeed if God closed the book on our life after we committed our first sin. But happily this is not the case. The Old Testament (see Ps 31) and the New Testament (see Rom 3:20) bring out the reality and the universality of sin in order to reveal God's mercy which enables every individual sinner to repent and return to him. And this mercy of God was revealed by Jesus himself in his actions (Lk 7:47-50) and in the parables of the lost sheep and the prodigal son (Lk 15:1-32). Thus, the revelation of God's merciful love throughout the Old Testament leads up to Jesus, the incarnate revelation of the Father's redeeming love. Jesus, then, can and does free us from the slavery of sin and brings us back to share his life.

But we cannot receive God's mercy without conversion on our part. We must desire to turn away from sin and return to him. The Greek term used in the Bible for "conversion" means a complete change of direction, a transformation of ourselves and our way of life.

Our sins, then, are cleansed in the blood of Christ. "This is the cup of my blood, the blood of the new and everlasting covenant. It will be shed for you and for all men so that sins may be forgiven" (Prayer at the Consecration in the Mass). Christ's redeeming death is the great act and proof of God's love for us. All forgiveness of sins therefore flows from Christ's sacrifice.

Baptism is the primary sacrament of repentance and the remission of sin. By it Christ brings us into his paschal mystery, causing us to die to sin and to live for God. How then are sins committed after Baptism to be forgiven?

When the life of the Spirit has been lost by mortal sins, it cannot be regained nor the divine forgiveness bestowed except by certain sacraments, or at least the desire for them. Even though the Eucharist contains the very source of the remission of sin, Christ's sacrifice, it is not through the Eucharist that we receive forgiveness for mortal sins. (We are excluded from Communion if we have unforgiven mortal sins on our conscience.) There are two sacraments designed precisely for spiritual healing: the sacrament of Penance and the sacrament we now call the Anointing of the Sick.

These two we call the sacraments of renewal. Penance renews Christ's life within us; this is its primary purpose. The Anointing of the Sick has a penitential effect, distinct from that of absolution but completing and sometimes substituting for it.

In the following pages we will treat these two sacraments of renewal.

Chapter 5
Penance (Reconciliation):
Called Back to the Father's Love

That the praise and worship of the Lord depend on the transformation of our lives by the healing and reconciling grace of God should be evident from the place of importance given to the sacraments in the life of the Church. The New Rite of Penance which was implemented in 1975 is a dominant feature of the sacramental renewal initiated by the Second Vatican Council. Its various options, its three different rites, its emphasis on Scripture and prayerful dialogue are clear indications that the ministry of the Church is one of healing, forgiveness, and reconciliation.

When Jesus walked the earth, he not only exhorted men to repentance so that they should abandon their sins and turn wholeheartedly to the Lord but he also welcomed sinners and reconciled them with the Father. He said to the paralytic, "Have courage, son, your sins are forgiven" (see Mt 9:1-8). Of Mary Magdalene he said: "That is why her many sins are forgiven — because of her great love" (Lk 7:47). These are only two of the many times he showed utmost concern for sinners. He died for our sins and rose again for our justification.

After his Resurrection he sent the Holy Spirit upon the apostles, empowering them to forgive or retain sins and sending them forth to all peoples to preach repentance and the forgiveness of sins in his name. "Receive the Holy Spirit. If you forgive men's sins, they are forgiven them" (Jn 20:23).

By giving to his apostles and their successors the power to forgive sin, Jesus instituted in his Church the sacrament of Penance. Thus, the faithful who fall into sin after Baptism may be reconciled with God and renewed in grace. The Church "possesses both water and tears: the water of Baptism, the tears of Penance," as St. Ambrose wrote centuries ago.

Although the Church herself is holy — Christ "loved the Church and gave himself up for her to make her holy" (Eph 5:25-26) — her members unfortunately often fall into sin. She therefore is always in need of purification and must constantly pursue repentance and renewal. The entire season of Lent is a yearly reminder of repentance, and the penitential rite at the beginning of every Mass constantly recalls our need for renewal.

In the sacrament of Penance, the faithful "obtain from the mercy of God pardon for their sins against him; at the same time they are reconciled with the Church which they wounded by their sins and which works for their conversion by charity, example, and prayer" *(Constitution on the Church,* 11).

By sin we offend God and suspend friendship with him. Hence, "the ultimate purpose of Penance is that we should love God deeply and commit ourselves completely to him" (see *Constitution on the Church,* 11). Therefore, the sinner who embraces Penance comes back to the Father who loved us into being, to Christ who gave himself up for us, and to the Holy Spirit who has been poured out on us abundantly.

But just as the holiness of one benefits others, so the sin of one harms others. Personal penance then demands reconciliation with those who have been wounded by one's sins. As we express sorrow to God, so too we should express sorrow to God's children.

People frequently join together to commit injustice; it is therefore only fitting that they aid each other in doing penance. The penitential celebrations which we will describe later are excellent ways of doing this. United in voice and spirit, the People of God pray to the Father "to forgive us our sins as we forgive those who sin against us."

In the life of individuals and of the community the wounds of sin are varied and multiple. The healing which Penance provides is likewise varied. Through Penance those who by grave sin have refused to return God's love are called back to the life they have lost. And those who through daily weakness fall into venial sins draw strength from another celebration of Penance to gain the full freedom of the children of God.

The faithful must confess to a priest each and every grave sin which they remember upon examination of their conscience. Moreover, frequent and careful celebration of this sacrament is also very useful as a remedy for venial sins.

Not a mere ritual repetition or psychological exercise, this is a serious striving to perfect the grace of Baptism so that, as we bear in our body the death of Jesus Christ, his life may be seen in us more clearly. The purpose of such a confession is to help us to conform more closely to Christ and to follow the voice of the Spirit more attentively.

<h1 style="text-align:center">I</h1>

ESSENTIAL PARTS OF PENANCE

Conversion to God with one's whole heart has always been the purpose of this sacrament. This conversion embraces sorrow for sin and the intent to lead a new life. It is expressed through confession made to the Church, due penance, and amendment of life. God grants pardon for sin through the ministry of the Church. The priest, acting in her name, absolves from sin in the name of the Father, and of the Son, and of the Holy Spirit.

Sorrow for sin implies a profound change of the whole person by which one begins to consider, judge, and arrange one's life according to the holiness and love of God. The authenticity of Penance depends on this heartfelt contrition.

Sorrow is necessary because sin destroys or weakens our friendship with God, ruins or hinders our relationship with others, and upsets the beauty and harmony of the world around us. Considering these consequences of sin, it is not too difficult to be truly sorry. Being human, resolving to avoid sin in the future is a different matter. However, it is enough to resolve here and now to do our best to stay away from sin.

Proper confession of sin arises from true knowledge of self before God and from contrition for sins so discovered. But any examination of conscience and accusation of sin should be made in the light of God's mercy. The penitent opens his/her heart to the minister of God; the minister, acting in the person of Christ, listens understandingly, advises wisely, and proposes an appropriate penance.

Penance (satisfaction or atonement) for sin is achieved by amendment of conduct and by reparation of injury. As to kind and extent, the priest will suit it to the personal condition of each penitent. It acts as a remedy for sin and help to renewal of life. Thus the penitent, forgetting the past, again becomes part of the mystery of salvation and turns bravely toward the future.

The sacrament of Penance is completed by the *sign of absolution* in which God grants pardon to the penitent. The words and actions of the minister are visible signs of God's loving kindness. The father receives the repentant son (Lk 15:11-32), Christ places the lost sheep on his shoulders and brings it back to the sheepfold (Lk 15:1-7), and the Holy Spirit sanctifies this temple of God again or lives more fully within it.

II
REVISED RITES OF PENANCE

In its *Constitution on the Liturgy* the Second Vatican Council decreed that "the rite and formulas of Penance are to be revised in such a way that they may more clearly express the nature and effects of this sacrament." This revision was completed in 1974 and implemented in 1975. The document contained three revised forms for the celebration of the sacrament and also a form for nonsacramental penitential services called "penitential celebrations."

The revised rites brought back into prominence the term "reconciliation," which describes the liturgical action as an encounter of mercy between God and penitent. The word "penance" looks more to the actions of the penitent — confession of sins, sorrow for sins, and atonement (penance) for sins.

The purpose of this revision was to remind the faithful of the importance of this sacrament of healing and to move them to more fervent service of God and neighbor. When we confess our sins with proper dispositions, we share in the sacrament itself. The priest, in the name of Christ, completes the sacrament with the words of forgiveness. Thus, as we experience and proclaim the mercy of God in our lives, we celebrate with the priest the liturgy by which the Church continually renews itself.

It was hoped that this renewal would encourage the use of

a sacrament that had for various reasons fallen into neglect. At first, it seemed that this revision would not stem the tide of infrequent confessions. People were hesitant about using the new forms prescribed, especially the option of confessing face-to-face with the priest. However, as time went on they began to realize that the changes were not all that drastic.

People came to understand that the basic elements of Penance remained the same: they still had to confess their sins, be sorry for them, and do penance for them. Once they became accustomed to the variation in the external rites they found them very helpful, actually making their confessions much easier. And those who confessed face-to-face were pleased with this much more personal approach. All in all, the revised rites impressed penitents with the necessity of internally disposing themselves for the celebration of this sacrament.

The reconciliation of penitents may be celebrated at any time on any day, but the people should be informed (by bulletin or other means) of designated times for confessions. Advent and Lent, of course, are most appropriate seasons for celebrating the sacrament and for nonsacramental penitential services.

Three revised rites for the sacrament are now in use: a) for individual penitents; b) for several penitents with individual confession and absolution; and c) for a large group of people with general confession and absolution. Also, penitential celebrations have become quite popular. The first of these rites we will consider in more detail, since this is the ordinary way in which a penitent confesses. The rest will be described only briefly here.

Reconciliation of Individual Penitents

The external changes in this form of Penance create a greater sense of ease and informality. This is clearly seen when penitents opt for the "reconciliation room." There, seated in a chair, they speak face-to-face with the priest. Those who exercise this option have found the quiet dignity of the room itself to be a great aid in making their confessions a happy, peaceful meeting in faith with the merciful Jesus. And those who choose to confess behind a screen have also found the new format of confession a more liberating experience.

PREPARATION: Before going to confession, penitents should prepare themselves by a prayer to ask the guidance of the Holy Spirit. Then they examine their conscience by checking their lives against the commandments of God and the precepts of the Church. They should recall the motives for contrition: the goodness, holiness, and justice of God, the sufferings of Christ, and the malice of sin. At the same time they should awaken a firm resolve, with God's help, to avoid sin and the causes of sin in the future.

CONFESSION: On entering the confessional or reconciliation room, the penitent is greeted by the priest in a kind and brotherly way. The person then makes the sign of the cross, saying: *"In the name of the Father, and of the Son, and of the Holy Spirit. Amen."*

The priest then invites the penitent to confidence in God with these or similar words: "May God, who gives light to our hearts, grant you to know your sins in truth and recognize his mercy."

The person answers: *"Amen."*

At this point, the priest or penitent may read a text from Holy Scripture which proclaims the mercy of God and calls the penitent to repentance. This reading is optional.

Now the actual confession begins. The penitent introduces him/herself: "Father, I'm single (married, widow, widower, divorced); my last confession was (so many days, weeks, months, years ago)." School children usually mention the grade they are in. Then, if customary the penitent says: "I confess to almighty God, etc." Otherwise, all that is needed are these or similar words: "These are my sins." If mortal sins are confessed, they should be told as to number, kind, and circumstance which might change the nature of the sin. It is not necessary but useful to confess venial sins, especially those which are most frequent and most troublesome to oneself and others.

If necessary, the priest will help the penitent make his/her confession. He will give suitable counsel and instruction and urge sorrow for sin and amendment of life. If the penitent has been the source of harm or scandal to others, he/she must resolve to make reparation.

The priest then imposes a penance. This will correspond to the seriousness and the nature of the sins confessed. It may consist of prayer, self-denial, or works of service to others.

Next the penitent expresses sorrow for sin and resolves to begin a new life. This may be done in various ways: use the words of the traditional Act of Contrition, use one's own words to formulate an act of sorrow, or use these words or others like them:

My God, I am sorry for my sins with all my heart. In choosing to do wrong and failing to do good, I have sinned against you whom I should love above all things. I firmly intend, with your help, to do penance, to sin no more, and to avoid whatever leads me to sin. Our Savior Jesus Christ suffered and died for us. In his name, my God, have mercy.

ABSOLUTION: After this prayer, the priest holds his hands over the head of the penitent (or at least extends his right hand) and pronounces the form of absolution.

The penitent now listens prayerfully to the words of forgiveness.

After the absolution, the priest says: "Give thanks to the Lord, for he is good."

And the penitent responds: *"His mercy endures forever."* Then the priest dismisses the penitent in these or similar words: "The Lord has freed you from your sins. Go in peace."

On leaving the confessional, the penitent says his/her penance immediately; or (if it is to be an act of self-denial or a work of service), he/she makes plans to do it as soon as possible.

Reconciliation of Several Penitents
with Individual Confession and Absolution

The second form of the sacrament of Penance is designed to show the community aspect of reconciliation. When a

number of penitents assemble for confession it is fitting that
they be prepared by a celebration of the Word of God. Here is
a brief description of the service.

This rite begins with a psalm, antiphon, or other
appropriate song. Then the priest speaks briefly about the
importance and purpose of the celebration and the order of
the service. He invites all to pray in silence, after which he
sings or says a suitable prayer.

The celebration of the Word now takes place, after which a
period of silence follows. This gives each one the chance to
absorb the message and heartily assent to it.

A homily based on the text of the reading (or readings) is
now given. This should lead the penitents to examine their
consciences and renew their lives. A communal examination of conscience and awakening of contrition may take the
place of the homily. This is done with brief considerations
adapted to the background, age, and state of life of those
assembled.

The rite of reconciliation now begins. All are invited to
kneel or bow their heads, and to join in a common prayer,
such as *"I confess to almighty God."* Standing, they sing an
appropriate song. The Lord's Prayer is always added at the
end.

Next the penitents go to the priests designated for
individual confession. After confessing their sins, they are
offered suitable counsel, given a fitting act of penance, and
are absolved from their sins.

After the confessions have been heard, all are invited to
offer thanks and to do good works which will proclaim the
grace of repentance in the life of the entire community and
each of its members. They then sing a song of praise or join
together in an appropriate prayer. The priest now concludes
the common prayer and blesses the assembly — which
blessing is responded to with the words: *"Thanks be to God."*

Reconciliation by
General Confession and Absolution

When it is physically or morally impossible to make an
individual, integral confession, it is lawful and even

necessary for the priest to give general absolution to a group of people. This is evident in cases involving danger of death — on the battlefield, for example. But it is also lawful when there is grave need. For example, if there are not sufficient confessors to hear the individual confessions of a number of penitents who would, through no fault of their own, be deprived of sacramental grace or Holy Communion for a long time, general absolution may be given.

This may happen especially in mission territories where people often go for months — even years — without seeing a priest. But it may also happen in other places. And where a grave need is established, priests — following the guidelines of their bishop — may give general absolution.

In order to receive general absolution penitents must properly dispose themselves and carefully fulfill certain conditions. They should be sorry for their sins and resolve to avoid committing them again. They should plan to repair any scandal and harm they may have caused; they should resolve to confess in due time each one of the grave sins which they cannot confess individually under the present circumstances.

Unless they are impeded by a just reason, those who receive general absolution from grave sins should go to individual confession before receiving this kind of absolution again. They are strictly bound, unless this is morally impossible, to confess within a year. Obviously, they too are bound by the general precept of confessing at least once a year all grave sins which they have not individually confessed before.

Here is a brief description of the rite used under the above circumstances. Everything is done as in the reconciliation of several penitents with individual absolution except for the following changes.

After the homily, or as part of it, the priest reminds the assembly to repent of their sins, to promise to amend their lives, to repair any scandal and harm caused by their sins, and to confess individually at the proper time each of the serious sins which cannot now be confessed. He then proposes a general penance.

Next he invites them to indicate by some sign (kneeling down or bowing their heads, for example) that they wish to receive absolution.

The penitents then express a general formula for confession (*"I confess to almighty God,"* for example). A prayer or appropriate song may now be said or sung, and the Lord's Prayer is always added at the end.

Then, holding his hands over them, he gives absolution, and invites all to thank God and to acknowledge his mercy. Finally, after a suitable song, he blesses and dismisses them.

Penitential Celebrations

In order to foster a communal spirit of penance, penitential celebrations may be (and should be) held from time to time. These can be an aid in the preparation for individual confession at a later time. They can especially help children gradually to form their conscience about sin and to learn about freedom from sin through the mercy of Jesus Christ. Penitential celebrations can also be designed to assist catechumens (those under instructions to become Catholics) understand the importance of reconciliation and the need for constant conversion. Care should be taken, however, that these services are not confused with the celebration of the sacrament of Penance.

These celebrations (or services) are similar to but distinct from the last two rites described above. They follow the general format of these two celebrations; but though forgiveness is present there is neither confession of sins nor absolution from the priest. Their structure is as follows.

God's Word invites all to conversion and renewal of life and announces freedom from sin through the death and Resurrection .of Christ. Before or after the readings from Scripture, selections from the Fathers or other writers may be read.

After the homily and reflection on God's Word, the congregation unites in voice and spirit with some prayer suited to general participation. Then, at the end of the Lord's Prayer the priest concludes with a prayer and dismisses the people.

These penitential celebrations are also very useful in places where no priest is available for regular confession. (A Sister, Brother, catechist, or lay person may lead the service.) They offer aid in reaching that perfect contrition which comes from charity and they enable the participants to obtain God's grace through a desire for the sacrament of Penance.

III
PROBLEMS WITH PENANCE

Despite the beauty of the sacrament of reconciliation as outlined in the preceding pages, problems still exist in the minds of many. The number of penitents who make use of this sacrament is in decline. Why?

One reason may be a resistance to change — not just to the revised form of Penance but also to the fact that people no longer can fall back on a clear-cut morality. (So many things are being questioned these days.) But perhaps the real reason is an understandable reaction against the way this sacrament has often been celebrated in the past.

On the part of penitents this could arise from poor instruction when they were young. Some still confess like second graders. They have never adapted their manner of confessing to their present age and condition. Some, too — because of certain circumstances — have forgotten how to confess. And because they no longer remember the "magic" formula, they stay away. Others, recalling the long lines of penitents, the sometimes grouchy, heavy-handed confessor, the impersonal absolution, and the customized penance, look back on the sacrament as an embarrassing, often painful experience. Still others retain their childhood fear of confession: harrowing memories of an unlighted box-like room, a ghostly figure on the other side of a dark screen, probing questions asked, and hesitant answers given. But most of all, in the hearts of many there remains that basic fear common to all of us: fear caused by the embarrassment and humiliation of revealing to another the faults of which we are guilty.

On the part of confessors, this reluctance to confess could arise from the routine way many priests celebrate the sacrament, the refusal of some even to offer advice and consolation to the penitent, and the hesitancy of others to do away with customized penances and substitute a positive penance (like an act of charity) to atone for sin.

Of course there are many other reasons why confession is not popular these days, but perhaps much doubt will be eliminated by answering the age-old question: Why must sins be confessed to a priest? This is answered in John 20:20-23 where Jesus commissioned his apostles to forgive sin, or refuse to forgive — when a person is not properly disposed. But a priest cannot do this unless the sins are told to him in the first place.

It is true that some people expect too much of the priest — as if he were a degreed counselor or psychologist. But the penitent rightfully expects the priest to be prayerful, emotionally mature, loving, faith-filled, wise and understanding. Such a priest will listen willingly, will not be afraid to bestow a healing touch, will be conscientious and yet willing to give penitents the benefit of a doubt, and will be dignified in his use of the sacramental words and symbols — knowing that in this celebration he represents Christ, the Healer.

With improvement on both the part of the priest and the penitent, the revised rite of reconciliation can once more become what Jesus meant it to be — a personal (and joyful) encounter with the merciful Christ.

Someday — we hope very soon — every church will have at least one combination confessional-reconciliation room. Many churches already have such. The room has two sections divided by a floor-to-ceiling screen. The penitent's side has a kneeler and a comfortable chair. This confessional side is softly illuminated and the grate has large enough spaces for the penitent to see the priest. On the other side of the grate the priest sits in a brighter light before a table and a conveniently placed chair for those who wish to confess face-to-face.

On entering the room, the penitent has two choices. One may choose to sit or kneel and confess in absolute secrecy as in the past, or one may choose to sit at the table and confess face-to-face with the priest. Many are now choosing this latter approach. And though the first experience may have been somewhat trying for some, most continue to do so because the greater openness of such a confession makes it easier for them to concentrate on their personal attitudes toward their sins rather than on specific acts and routine lists of repeated sins.

A brief look at the revised rite will make it clear why this new approach will encourage more frequent and better use of Penance. By refashioning the externals of this sacrament, the Church has allowed the Father's love and forgiveness to shine through. Our life is a pilgrimage, a going home. We have to continue the process of conversion. Learning how to be true sons and daughters of God takes time and courage. To aid in this, the rite is shaped by Scripture and filled with opportunities for shared prayer.

After a prayer for light and courage you, the penitent, examine your conscience. How long ago was your last confession? What sins have you committed in that period? (You may have sinned in what you did or what you failed to do; and sins may occur in thought, word, or action.)

Serious sins — major wrongs committed with full awareness and total freedom — will be recognized without much effort. These should be confessed together with any major circumstances which notably change the kind of sin it was (for example, to steal from church adds a sin of sacrilege to the sin of theft). The approximate number of times the sin was committed must also be mentioned. Lesser sins — since they can be forgiven by a prayer of sorrow and by Communion — need not be confessed. However, to confess at least some of them helps you conquer those faults and grow into the kind of person God wants you to become.

Your examination should be honest. It is not a time for playing games; you must come to grips with what you know was wrong in the past. But, at the same time, you should not take too long or dig too deeply. Under ordinary circumstances, it should be sufficient to pinpoint your failures of love for God and neighbor as indicated in the Ten Commandments and in the precepts of the Church. But your main concern should be your attitude toward your life as a Christian, as a Catholic. Are you trying to grow in the life of the Spirit through prayer, reading and meditating on the Word of God, receiving the sacraments, giving good example, and practicing self-denial? (These are all positive aspects of the sacrament too often forgotten.) Penance heals, yes; but it also fosters God-like living — for those who understand what Christianity is all about.

If you have not received this sacrament for years, you should of course examine your conscience thoroughly. However, it is more practical to begin your confession with words to this effect, "Father, it's been two, three (whatever) years since my last confession. Please help me." Then the priest will ask about failures against the commandments and other relevant questions. All you have to do is to answer "no" or "yes" and give the approximate number of times the sins were committed.

Sorrow for your sins and determination to do better in the future should well up in you as you examine your conscience. Without this, no sin can be forgiven. You are now ready to enter the confessional or reconciliation room.

Regardless of the manner you choose to confess, the greeting you receive on entering is a clear indication of the dignified freedom fostered by this new approach. Priest and penitent greet each other as friends, not as judge and culprit.

You are not being "called on the carpet" to face an angry ruler. You are there to admit that you have lost (or weakened) your friendship with God; and to ask forgiveness of the Father through the ministry of one of his Son's healers. Healer the priest is, but like you he too is "wounded" by sin.

Because he is a friend, he understands your human weakness, and is most anxious to provide you with divine strength. And he does this by his sincerity of greeting, his concerned attitude as he listens, his expression as he reads the Scripture, his fervor as he prays the words of forgiveness, and his warmth in saying good-by. Some of this can be perceived through a screen, but it is most obvious to the penitent who confesses face-to-face in a reconciliation room. Such a confessor is a true friend.

Sample Confessions

For your convenience, here are two sample confessions. Each one eliminates the old style "laundry-list approach" in the telling of sins, and emphasizes the "growth attitude approach."

A. "Forgive me, Father. I'm a married woman. It's been two months since my last confession. I got angry and lost my temper with my children and my husband several times. When things start going wrong in the morning, they pile up the rest of the day. And then I lose control — taking it out on the kids, and my husband when he comes home.

"I know this is selfish. My anger just makes things worse. I'll try not to take out my own frustrations on others. But where should I start, Father? Have you any advice?"

B. "Help me, Father, to make a good confession. I'm a fifth grade boy, and it has been one month since my last confession.

"I'm always getting into fights with another boy in my class. Just now in church, I think I figured out why. We're both pretty good in school, but on the playground he always seems to do better than I do. I guess I'm jealous.

"I'm sorry for this sin and I'll really try not to be jealous any more."

When we confess in this honest and meaningful way we insure our spiritual growth and development. The grace (God-presence) that comes to us in this sacrament helps us to grow. Growth of any kind is a gradual and constant process. But it is also a process that does not proceed automatically along the right lines. It must be coaxed along and guided. Confession at regular intervals — say, once a month — motivated by love for Christ and the children of God, not by anxiety and fear, can insure our growth as Christians.

Each time we confess in the way described here we renew our dedication to Christ. We rededicate ourselves as members of the People of God. We learn to see ourselves not simply as individuals struggling on our own but as apostles whose care it is to build up God's family. Regular confession will keep us from drifting through life. It programs for us personal encounters with Christ himself, and at the same time keeps us from becoming indifferent to Christ in our brothers and sisters.

Penance, Reconciliation. Come celebrate! Experience the bittersweet joy of forgiveness!

Chapter 6
Anointing of the Sick:
Strength for Soul, Mind, and Body

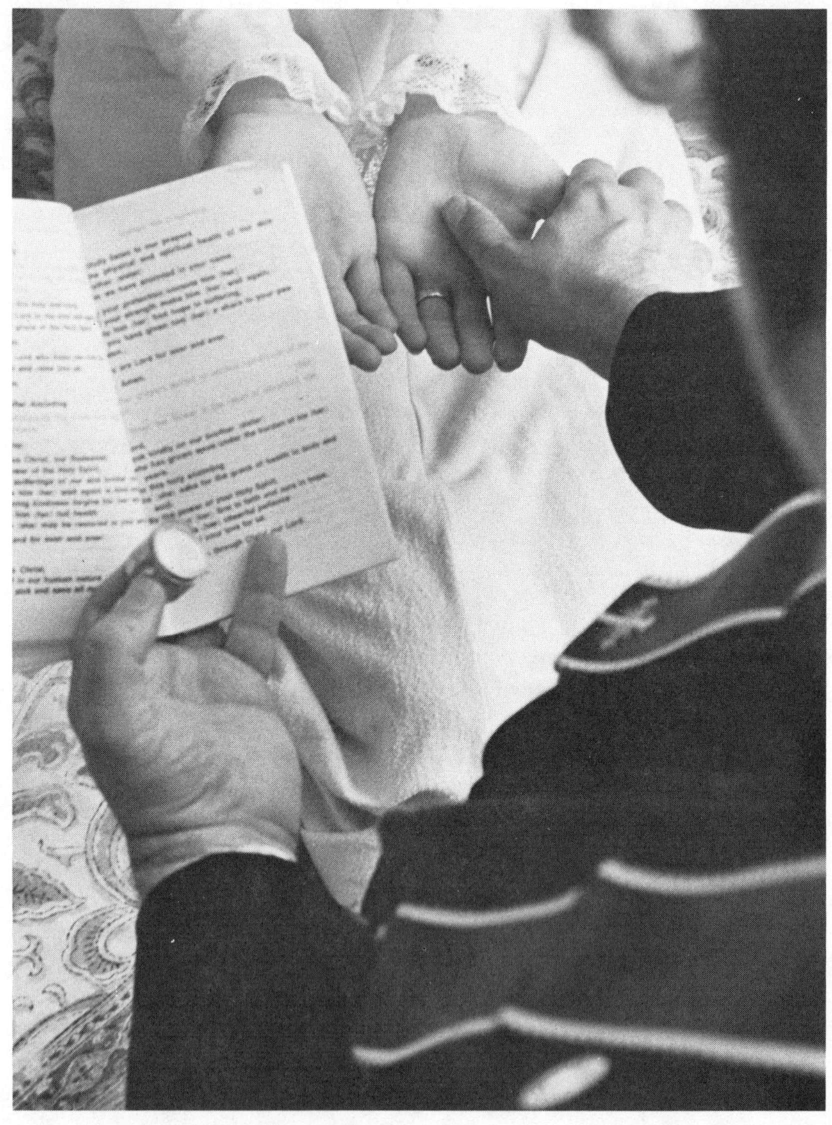

In the third chapter of the *Constitution on the Sacred Liturgy* issued by the Second Vatican Council we read the following:

"The purpose of the sacraments is to sanctify men, to build up the body of Christ, and finally, to give worship to God. Because they are signs they also instruct . . ." (59).

The document goes on to say that over the passage of time the meaning and purpose of the sacraments had become less clear to the faithful as certain features crept into the rituals. And so the Council decreed certain principles for the revision of the sacraments: The language of the people was to be used, and new rituals were to be drawn up.

The *Constitution* then speaks of the individual sacraments, and devotes three paragraphs to the sacrament of Extreme Unction:

"Extreme Unction, which may also and more fittingly be called *Anointing of the Sick,* is not a sacrament for those only who are at the point of death. Hence, as soon as any one of the faithful begins to be in danger of death from sickness or old age, the appropriate time for him to receive this sacrament has certainly already arrived.

"In addition to the separate rites for Anointing of the Sick and for Viaticum, a continuous rite shall be prepared according to which the sick man is anointed after he has made his confession and before he receives Viaticum.

"The number of the anointings is to be adapted to the occasion, and the prayers accompanying the rite of anointing are to be revised so as to correspond with the varying conditions of the sick who receive the sacrament" (73-75).

It was to put these decrees of the Council into effect that the new ritual for the sacrament of the Anointing of the Sick was issued in the fall of 1972, and took effect on January 1, 1974. No longer is the sacrament called "Extreme Unction," or "Last Anointing"; it is the anointing and pastoral care of the *sick.* Certainly in the popular mind this sacrament had, over the years, lost that dimension of care for the sick. As the practice of medicine developed into a true science, the doctor was the person summoned to care for the sick; only when his skill failed was the priest called for. Thus the sacramental anointing was seen as a herald of impending and sure death, and its administration was held off until the sick person was truly on his deathbed, with no hope of recovery.

TEACHING OF THE CHURCH

But the anointing of the sick was always meant, in the mind of Christ and of the Church, to be a sacrament, an encounter with Christ, for those whose illness entailed a danger of death. The Council of Trent (1551) correctly made the distinction between *danger* of death and *point* of death; it was never the teaching of the Church to postpone the anointing until the point of death had been reached.

Despite this, however, the tradition of waiting too long before calling the priest to attend the sick continues even to the present time. It is hoped that the new name for this sacrament — anointing and pastoral care of the sick — will remind everyone to call the priest as soon as there is *danger* of death from sickness or old age.

Just what is the basis for the teaching of the Church with regard to this sacrament? Two passages in the New Testament refer to the anointing of the sick: "They expelled many demons, anointed the sick with oil, and worked many cures" (Mk 6:13). "Is there anyone sick among you? He should ask for the presbyters of the Church. They in turn are to pray over him, anointing him with oil in the Name of the Lord. This prayer uttered in faith will reclaim the one who is ill, and the Lord will restore him to health. If he has committed any sins, forgiveness will be his" (Jas 5:14-15).

These quotations must be seen in the context of Jesus' mission as Messiah, as the anointed one (the Christ) who was to fulfill the prophecies of the Old Testament concerning the kingdom of God. This kingdom is not of this world (Jn 18:36), yet it begins in this world. Sin had resulted in sickness, suffering, and death. Jesus healed the sick as a sign that sin had been overcome (Mk 2:10-11), and with sin, its effects. Jesus, then, was a genuine faith-healer. He healed sick bodies as well as sinful souls. His healing miracles are signs that the kingdom has arrived — the sick are made well, and all who witness these cures are offered the gift of faith, conversion, and ultimately eternal life. The kingdom which Jesus has already established will reach its completion on the day of his Second Coming, with the resurrection of all mankind.

The apostles continued the healing mission of Jesus, as he told them to do: "Then he summoned his twelve disciples and gave them authority . . . to cure sickness and disease of every kind" (Mt 10:1). And the directive found in the letter of St. James, which was practiced from early Christian times, speaks of the healing of a Christian who is seriously ill, but by no means dying. These cures, however, should not be seen as something purely medical; in the thought of those times, there was no distinction between body and soul — man was seen as one. They saw a relationship between sickness and sin, and so the prayer and anointing was seen as ministering to the whole man, bringing him what we would call both bodily and spiritual healing.

Oil used for physical healing was something very real to the people of the early Church. It is, for example, one of the remedies applied by the Good Samaritan to the wounds of the man he found lying by the wayside (Lk 10:34). And even modern medicine uses liniments with an oil base.

HISTORY OF ANOINTING

For at least the first eight centuries of her existence, the Church used the anointing as a rite for the sick. The oil to be used was blessed by the bishop, but the anointing of the sick person was done not only by the presbyters (priests) but also by lay people, who would anoint themselves or a sick relative or friend with the oil which the bishop had blessed. This anointing seems to have been accompanied by a prayer and the laying on of hands.

The oldest complete ritual for anointing which we have today dates from the time of Charlemagne, around the year 815. Here we see the sacrament as a communal celebration involving various ministers, a choir, and members of the local church.

But it was at this time that the anointing began to undergo a transformation — from a sacrament of the sick to a sacrament of the dying. Anointing by lay persons was abolished, and a renewal of the priestly ministry was begun. One effect of this renewal was the compilation, perhaps for the first time, of rites and prayers to be used by the priests — a book of ritual. Unfortunately, when this book was assembled, the rite for anointing was placed right after the section on deathbed Penance. This resulted in a confusion of the two sacraments; and the remission of sins was seen as a principal effect of the anointing. The anointing became a sacrament of the dying, and the original order of administering the sacraments had changed — from confession, anointing, and Communion (called Viaticum or "Food for the journey") to confession, Viaticum, and anointing. Thus the anointing became, in reality, the "last" rite.

This changing view of the sacrament reached its completion with the work of the scholastic theologians in the thirteenth century. Rather than referring to the evidence of earlier practices, they concentrated on the meaning of the anointing as it was administered in their day — as a sacrament for the dying, the primary effect of which was spiritual. For they saw the sacraments as means of conferring grace, and were unable to see how the anointing, or any sacrament, could have any effect on the physical health of a person. The cure brought about by the sacrament was the remission of sin, and the anointing became a sacrament of the dying whose purpose was to prepare the soul for immediate entrance into heaven.

The Council of Trent saw the grace of anointing as a grace of the Holy Spirit with corresponding spiritual, physical, and psychological benefits. It rejected the opinion that the anointing was "only" for the dying in favor of a statement that it was a sacrament "especially" for the dying: "This anointing is to be administered to the sick, especially those who are in such a condition as to appear to have reached the end of their life."

The words "especially for the dying" have been emphasized since the time of Trent. No doubt, this has been the main reason why people waited till the last minute before calling the priest to the bedside of the sick. But in recent years more attention has been paid to the phrase, "This anointing is to be administered to the sick." For this reason, the *Constitution on the Liturgy* says quite plainly, "Anointing of the Sick is not a sacrament for those only who are at the point of death. Hence, as soon as any one of the faithful begins to be in danger of death from sickness or old age, the appropriate time for him to receive this sacrament has certainly already arrived" (73).

PURPOSE OF THE SACRAMENT

Thus, today, we see that the sacrament is a sacrament for the sick. No longer is the point of death a condition for its reception; the revised ritual teaches us the meaning of the sacrament. We read in the blessing of the oil: "May your blessing come upon all who are anointed with this oil, that they may be freed from pain and illness and made well again in body, mind, and soul."

Why does Christ offer this sacrament to those who are sick? To answer this question we must consider what serious illness is and what effect it has on persons. Illness means more than pain and physical suffering. Serious illness brings with it depression — a feeling of isolation from others, especially from the family — because it makes persons preoccupied with themselves and their sickness. It causes impatience, discouragement, at times despair. Once independent individuals now experience a painful dependence on others, even for the most basic of bodily needs and functions. Communication can break down, and the sick person often feels that no one really understands them or cares about them — even God.

It is to remedy this situation that the sacrament is administered. The anointing is not aimed merely at eternal salvation, nor only a physical healing and restoration to health. Rather it benefits the *whole* being of all who receive, overcoming the obstacles to grace and salvation which are a direct result of the sickness. It gives them an effective way to cope with their present life situation, and to integrate their illness into their life in a way that is truly Christian. It wants to heal each one of them as a body-soul unity. Whenever the sacrament is received in faith, we may look for an inner healing, a sacramental strengthening which leads believers, in spite of and even *through* their illness, to identify with their Savior, who suffered, died, and was raised up in response to the will of his Father.

Those who receive this sacrament worthily receive strength for soul, mind, and body, Of course, physical healing does not always take place, because this depends so much on how open they are to the power of God.

Those who are present at the anointing can also benefit greatly. Usually they are the ones who have been caring for the sick person. And sometimes they are amazed at what happens after this sacrament has been celebrated. Chronic complainers become uncomplaining patients, and proud persons learn the lessons of humility. These and other changes are not lost on those who minister to the sick.

Yes, the inner healing of the sick persons themselves gradually brings about a change of attitude and outlook. They come to realize just how interdependent we all are, how much we need one another, need to love and be loved. They can see others in a new light and enter into much deeper and more meaningful conversations with them, enabling them to speak of the deepest concerns of human life. The sacrament makes those who receive more aware of the concern which the Church, the community of believers, has for them, and gives them a feeling of unity and solidarity with their fellow Christians, all members of the Body of Christ.

And serious illness confronts persons with a basic and absolute fact of life — that death awaits each of us. Sick people begin to realize that they are finite. The sacrament of Anointing helps them to face up to this fact, helps them to examine and to clarify their own personal values. Strengthened by the Word of God and by this sacrament, they are enabled to accept their finiteness as something willed by the Father as the way to union with him.

SACRAMENT OF THE LIVING

The Anointing of the Sick is one of those sacraments which has traditionally been called a sacrament of the living; that is, it is to be received by those in the state of grace — those who have not broken off their relationship with God through serious sin. That is why there is a place in the ordinary rite of anointing for sacramental confession, before the anointing itself takes place. But if sick persons are unable to receive the sacrament of Penance (because they are unconscious, for example), the anointing would remit their sins.

All the sacraments are encounters with Christ, with his saving love and mercy. The Anointing of the Sick brings with it healing, forgiveness, and reconciliation. But in order that this encounter might be authentic, that these effects might be realized, it is necessary that there be true sorrow. Without that essential condition, there can be no forgiveness, whether through anointing or through the sacrament of Penance.

MODERN RITE

How is this sacrament administered according to the present ritual? The first thing that is pointed out is that the priest is to plan the ceremony according to the condition of the sick person; if possible, he is to do this planning with the person or other members of the family. If the sick person is not confined to bed, the sacrament may most fittingly be administered in a church, with a suitable chair prepared for the sick person, and opportunity for relatives and friends to take part in the ceremony.

The ceremony itself follows a format we have become familiar with, one similar to that used at Mass. There is first an introductory rite, in which the priest greets the sick person and others who are present. He may sprinkle them with holy water, recalling their Baptism by which they were joined with Christ in his death and Resurrection. Then, referring to the letter of St. James, the priest recalls the purpose of the sacrament — to "entrust our sick brother (sister) to the grace and power of Jesus Christ, that the Lord may ease his/her suffering and grant him/her health and salvation."

This introduction is followed by a penitential rite. If necessary, it is here that the sick person confesses his/her sins privately and receives absolution. Otherwise one of the penitential rites of the Mass is used — the confession of sin or the "Lord, have mercy." Then there is a reading from Scripture, chosen according to the circumstances and the condition of the sick person, and followed by a short homily on the reading and on the sacrament. After the homily there is a litany or series of petitions praying for the sick person.

Then the priest, in that ancient gesture of prayer and invocation of the power of the Holy Spirit, lays his hands on the head of the sick person in silence. This is a powerful moment, and recalls that healing touch which Jesus imparted so often during his ministry. Next the priest blesses the oil which is to be used for the anointing; or if it has already been blessed, he says a prayer of thanks over it.

The actual sacramental moment, the anointing, then follows. Using the oil, the priest anoints the sick person on the forehead and on the hands, while saying:

"Through this holy anointing may the Lord in his love and mercy help you with the grace of the Holy Spirit. Amen.

"May the Lord who frees you from sin save you and raise you up. Amen."

Through this action and these words, the sacrament of the Anointing of the Sick is administered.

The priest then offers a prayer chosen according to that person's situation. He asks the Lord to heal, or to help in acceptance of advanced age, or to help and welcome the person if he/she is about to die. All those present join together, as children of the Father, and pray the Lord's Prayer. Then Holy Communion is distributed, just as at Mass, and the priest says a prayer after Communion, asking that the body of Christ may renew the sick person. Finally the priest blesses those who are present.

ANOINTING AT MASS

It is most fitting, if the condition of the sick person permits, and especially if Communion is to be received, that the anointing take place during a celebration of Mass, either in a church, the person's home, or the hospital. Except on certain solemn feasts, the prayers and Scripture readings of the Mass for the sick are used. The sacrament is administered after the homily: there is the laying on of hands, the blessing of oil or prayer of thanks over it, and the anointing itself. The litany for the sick person is used as the prayer of the faithful, concluding with a special prayer for that person. Then the Mass continues with the presentation of gifts. All those who are present may receive Communion under both kinds, eating the bread of life and drinking from the cup of salvation.

The rite of anointing makes provision for the anointing of several persons in the same ceremony. This communal anointing is most fitting, for the sacraments are celebrations of the whole Church. Through such a service our solidarity with each other, our brotherly assistance and care are emphasized.

A typical communal anointing was recently held in St. Alphonsus Church in Grand Rapids, Michigan. All the sick and elderly parishioners were invited to receive the sacrament. Transportation was provided for those normally confined to their homes. Nurses were on hand in case they were needed. The people were given name tags as they entered the church, and seated in the pews leaving every other pew empty. In this way, they did not have to leave their places at all during the Mass — the priests walked through the pews for the laying on of hands, for the anointing, and for the distribution of the Eucharist.

After Communion, young girls from the parish gave carnations to those who had been anointed, and after the Mass they served punch and cookies to the people in their pews. One hundred and twenty-five persons were anointed that day in one of the most moving ceremonies that old church has ever seen. And words are insufficient to express what those persons felt as they received the sacrament. Many said that it was the most moving, most impressive service they had ever been to, and their tears proved it. They felt the presence of the Spirit there among them. Some were happy just for the chance to be in church again. It was a true parish celebration, as all the sacraments should be, bringing the people together.

PROCEDURE AT POINT OF DEATH

What of those who have reached the point of death? If possible, they should receive the sacrament of Penance, then be anointed, and finally be given *Viaticum,* which is *the* sacrament of the dying. This final reception of the Eucharist is "food for the journey," a special sign of their participation in the death of the Lord and his passage to the Father, the mystery which is celebrated in the Eucharist. If there is insufficient time for all three sacraments to be given, the person is to confess and receive *Viaticum* immediately.

It is clear that the sacrament of the Anointing of the Sick should be administered in good time, so that the sick person can receive its full benefits. But in case of sudden accident, persons who are unconscious may be anointed if one is reasonably sure that they would have asked for the sacrament were they conscious.

This sacrament, like the other sacraments, can never be administered to those who have died; the sacraments are for those who are living. If the priest is called to minister to a person who is already dead, he should pray for the dead person, asking God to forgive the person's sins and welcome him/her into the joys of the kingdom; but he is never to anoint a person who is obviously dead. If there is a doubt whether the person is dead, the priest may anoint conditionally, prefixing the words of anointing with the statement, "If you are alive, we pray . . . . "

WHAT YOU CAN DO

Certainly this real celebration of the sacrament is a change from the days when the family called the priest to minister at the deathbed. This modern rite emphasizes the importance of pastoral care for the sick. The prayers and scriptural texts are deliberately chosen to fit each individual occasion. Every action points to Christ's love for all.

This great sacrament of Christ should always be but one part of a much wider concern for the sick on the part of the Church. A true pastoral ministry to the sick would include frequent visits to the elderly and sick, offering them whatever assistance, support, or loving concern they may need. It means offering these members of the People of God the opportunity to participate in the sacramental life of the Church — to receive the Eucharist often, to be reconciled through Penance, to be anointed.

This ministry must involve more people than just the parish priest or the hospital chaplain; everyone who claims the title of Christian must be willing to continue Jesus' ministry to the sick and suffering, the elderly and neglected. Lay ministers of the Eucharist who bring Communion to shut-ins can incorporate the sick into parish life, and help them to share in the liturgical and sacramental life of that community.

Those who practice the corporal works of mercy are the caring ones who bring the love of Christ to the sick. They will never be faced with the possibility of uttering those embarrassing, damning words: "Lord, when did we see you ill, and not attend you in your need?" (Mt 25:44)

SACRAMENTS FOR A SPECIAL LIFE

Matrimony:
Sacrament of Christian Love

Holy Orders: Sacrament
of Ministerial Priesthood

The traditional way of listing the sacraments which we have followed in this book has the advantage of drawing attention to the various situations for which they were instituted.

Baptism, Confirmation, and the Eucharist — the three sacraments of initiation — have been presented here in the order in which an adult receives them. They establish us in the Christian state, even though they are not equally necessary to the salvation of each person. (Confirmation, for example, is not in itself indispensable to salvation, but it is called for by Baptism, which is incomplete without it.)

The sacraments of Reconciliation and the Anointing of the Sick then come to the aid of Christians who have sinned after Baptism. The first restores (or refurbishes) the Christ-life that has been lost (or weakened) by sin; the second, being a complement to Reconciliation, brings a grace proper to the state of illness.

Finally, there are two sacraments designed, not for the salvation of the individual, but for a social function in the Church: Matrimony and Holy Orders. These sacraments are indispensable to the Church, though not to each individual Christian. They are not designed for everyone since they form the structure of the Body (the Church) with its differing functions.

By the sacrament of Matrimony couples mirror the union of Christ and his Church, the community of the People of God with Christ the Head. From marriage comes the family, in which new citizens of human society are born. "By the grace of the Holy Spirit received in Baptism these are made children of God, thus perpetuating the People of God through the centuries. The family is, so to speak, the domestic Church" *(Constitution on the Church,* 11). Husband and wife therefore consecrate themselves to a special life in the sacrament of Matrimony.

"Those of the faithful who are consecrated by Holy Orders are appointed to feed the Church in Christ's name with the Word and the grace of God." These words (from *Constitution on the the Church,* 11) describe briefly the role of priests in the sacramental life of the Church. Thus the sanctity of the People of God is maintained and fostered by the sacred and ordained ministry. By dedicating themselves to the service of the People of God, priests are truly fathers in the spiritual sense. From birth to burial theirs is the care of their spiritual family.

These two sacraments, then — which we will treat in the following pages — each in its own but related way, exercise spiritual paternity. They are social sacraments instituted by Christ to insure throughout time the continuation of the Christian community.

Chapter 7
Matrimony:
Sacrament of Christian Love

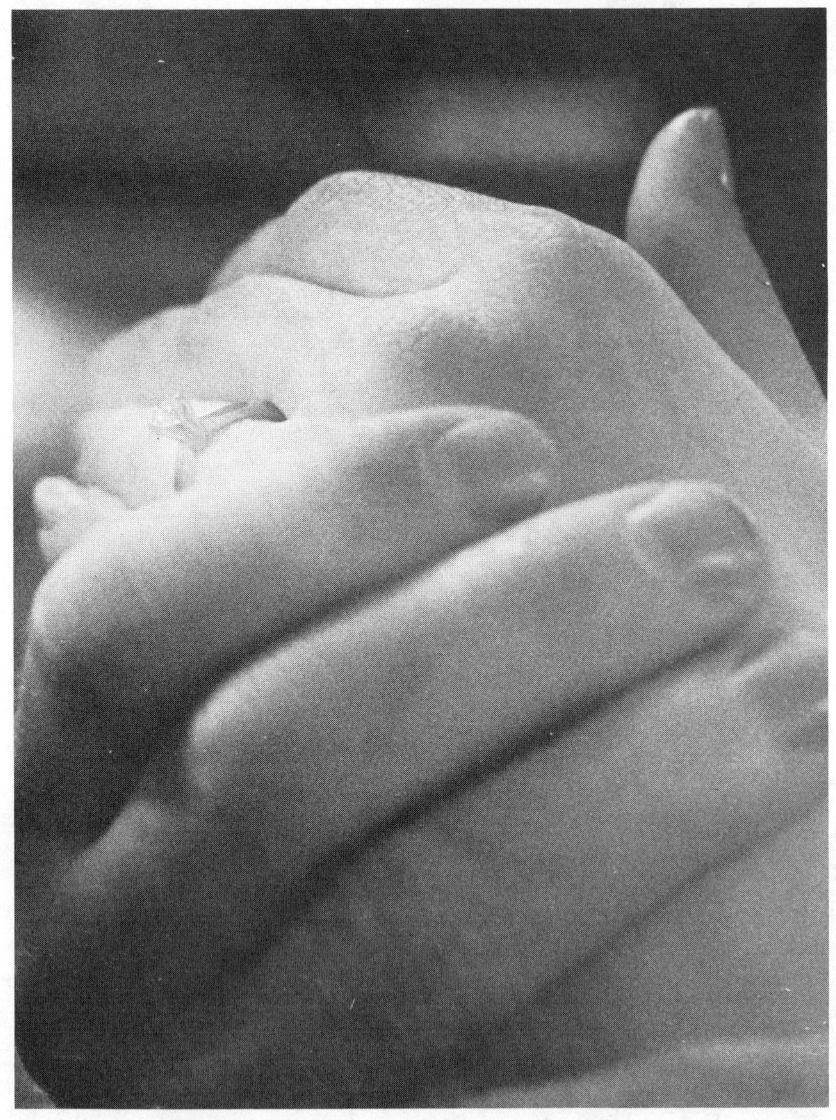

"It's impossible! I could never live up to those ideals or make such a commitment." That seems to be the reaction of many people today when they are confronted with the prospect of entering into or living a true Christian marriage. They find the challenge to be too great. What these people do not begin to realize is the breadth and depth of meaning to be found in the sacrament of Matrimony. They seem unaware of the great graces that come to the man and woman joined to one another and to Christ in this most holy of bonds.

In the few pages that follow it will be impossible to present all the elements that make up the sacrament of Christian Matrimony. Books much larger than this have been written on marriage and even on the individual areas of courtship, preparation for marriage, the marriage ceremony, married love, family living and other related topics. Hopefully these few pages will provide insights into Christian marriage. It would be even better if they would stimulate discussion or lead the reader to ask new questions, to look further into the subject or to consult a priest or religious educator for more information.

In an effort to be thorough and yet concise, four main areas will be considered: marriage as vocation, sacred institution, ceremony, and way of life. Following this the questions of mixed-faith marriage and marital failure will be considered briefly.

I
MARRIAGE AS VOCATION: A CALL TO HOLINESS

Each day in our life is filled with decisions. Will I have toast and coffee or bacon and eggs for breakfast? It's cloudy outside. Should I take my umbrella or should I take a chance on getting soaked on the way home? Every day we make many such decisions. Most of them are small and inconsequential and have little effect on daily life.

Some of our decisions are much more serious. They will affect us for years to come or even for the rest of our life. Should I go to college or get a job right after high school? What am I going to do with the rest of my life? Should I be a priest, Brother, Sister, stay single or get married? Decisions like this cannot be made overnight. Ideally, much thought should go into such major decisions. Other people should be consulted and the guidance of the Holy Spirit should be sought through prayer.

When it comes to the question of marriage, it seems that all too often these decision-making steps are not taken and people drift aimlessly into marriage. Instead of a genuine positive commitment to live one's life and attain holiness through the sacrament of Christian Matrimony, they simply decide to get married. Marriage becomes just another way of life and not the truly Christian calling to holiness that it should be.

God calls a person to the vocation of Christian marriage in the same way that he calls a young man to be a priest or Brother, or a woman to be a Sister. The dignity and holiness of the married state has been recognized ever more clearly in the 20th century. It is truly a sacred calling which has an important place in the Church. In an encyclical letter written in 1930 by Pope Piux XI, it states:

> Marriage must have as its higher and chief objective that of shaping and perfecting the interior life of husband and wife . . . . This persevering endeavor to bring each other to the state of perfection may be called the primary cause and reason of matrimony . . . when marriage is seen as a complete and intimate partnership and association.

This awareness of the dignity of the vocation of marriage grows in the coming decades and is further heightened in the documents which resulted from the Second Vatican Council in the mid 1960s. In the *Constitution on the Church* the bishops speak of the Christian vocation of marriage and its place in the Church.

> Christian spouses, in virtue of the sacrament of Matrimony whereby they signify and partake of the mystery of that unity and fruitful love which exists between Christ and the Church, help each other to attain to holiness in their married life and in the rearing and education of their children. By reason of their state

and way of life they have their own special gift among the People of God (11).

The document goes on to state that husbands and wives find their proper vocation in being witnesses of the faith and love of Christ to one another and to their children (35). Every Christian has received a call to holiness, but those called to live the sacrament of Matrimony have their own individual path to sanctity.

They should sustain one another in grace throughout the entire length of their lives. In this manner they offer all people the example of unwearying and generous love; in this way they build up the brotherhood in charity, in so doing they stand as witnesses and cooperators in the fruitfulness of Holy Mother Church (41).

It should be clear that marriage is much more than just something to do because most people get married at some time in their life. In Christian marriage Christ calls two baptized people together into an intimate union with each other and himself. By this sacramental sign they stand as witnesses to the world of the love which can exist between two people and the love which Christ has for his Church. Through the graces of this sacrament the married couple live their lives in love, always striving to deepen their union and to achieve the perfection of holiness to which they have been called by God.

Admittedly this is an ideal, yet it is something that each married couple must strive for every day of their married life. The Lord has called them to live this way and with his grace he will help them.

II
MARRIAGE AS INSTITUTION:
MADE SACRED BY GOD

To consider marriage as an institution is more sociological than theological, and yet the Church as it develops its theology of the sacrament of Matrimony must be aware of the social reality and must demonstrate a concern for the People of God in their present situation.

From the earliest days of mankind there has been a desire for offspring, for progeny who would live on after their parents had died. The family cared for the young and functioned as the chief unit of socialization. Throughout recorded history and around the world the family unit has taken various forms, but the monogamous (one man and one woman) union would seem to predominate in the Western world.

Within the monogamous unit there have been historical developments. For example the practice of freely choosing one's partner has arisen only recently, especially since the rise of industrialization and urbanization. The day of the matchmakers and the planned marriage is not that distant even in the United States. Marriages were formed for political, social, or economic reasons. Children were promised in marriage when they were still children. Many a bride saw her husband for the first time on the day of their wedding.

We can welcome the modern practice of free selection of marriage partners as a tremendous advancement, and yet it brings new problems to the institution of marriage. From the earliest fragments of the Old Testament to the most modern pronouncements on the sacrament of Matrimony, the Church has always attempted to provide inspiration and guidance to those who enter the state of marriage. This guidance has always been aimed to the people in their present life situation.

Old Testament

As early as the Book of Genesis we can find a reference to the ideals that are to be aspired to in a Christian marriage. After God has created man and woman to be companions to one another we read: "That is why a man leaves his father and mother and clings to his wife, and the two of them become one body" (Gn 2:24).

In actual fact it took many centuries before the people began to accept this standard for the institution of marriage. By today's standards the marriage practices of the people in the early Old Testament times were quite unenlightened.

Marriages were arranged by parents with little concern for the wishes of those being married. (Read Genesis 24 — the marriage of Isaac, or Genesis 38 — the story of Judah and Tamar.) A contract was often drawn up between the parties to determine the financial and property settlements coming from the marriage (read Tobit 7:16). From this marriage contract it was clear that the wife became the property of the husband and could be treated as he would treat any of his other worldly possessions.

It was not uncommon for a man to have children by another woman especially if his wife was unable to bear children. (Read Genesis 16 about Abraham and the slave girl.) The king could have his harem but was warned not to multiply wives in a cruel and unjust manner (see Dt 17:17). As late as the promulgation of the law code found in the Book of Deuteronomy (see Dt 21:15-17) it was still acceptable for a man to have two wives.

However in the later Old Testament writings (from the fifth century B.C.) a marriage of one man and one woman became the ideal and also the common practice. The praises of the good wife (read Sirach 26:1-4, 16-21) and the portrayal of the ideal wife (Proverbs 31:10-31) are best understood in the context of a permanent union between one man and one woman.

The most important contribution of the Old Testament to the Church's understanding of marriage was the idea of *covenant*. Covenant was the special agreement between God and his chosen people. (Read Genesis 17:3-22 for the covenant between God and Abraham, and Exodus 19 and 20 for the covenant with Moses.) This relationship of God and his people characterized by total love and service became the basic inspiration for the permanent and exclusive style of Christian marriage between husband and wife. From the teachings of the New Testament through the most modern Christian teachings about marriage, the covenant has remained as the basic model.

New Testament

The teachings of Jesus were primarily concerned with the permanence and indissolubility of marriage (Mt 19:3-12). In this pronouncement Jesus reaffirms what was said long ago in Genesis 2:24 about the husband and wife becoming one body. Jesus also repeated the caution against adultery and extended this to prohibit even looking lustfully at another woman (Mt 5:27-28).

It was left to the writers of the various Epistles to present the fuller teachings of the early Church toward marriage. Both Peter and Paul instruct the faithful in the requirements for Christian marriage. Reading 1 Peter 3:1-7, Colossians 3:18-21 and Titus 2:4-5 can provide inspiration and offer Christian marital ideals for husbands and wives as well as parents and children. In the entire seventh chapter of 1 Corinthians, Paul answers questions addressed to him about marriage, sexuality and virginity. He repeats the teachings of Jesus and expresses what must be considered as the doctrine of the early Church in regard to these matters.

The understanding of marriage as a sacrament comes most clearly from Ephesians 5:21-33. Paul says that the love of man and woman shown in Christian marriage must be a sign of the love of Christ for the Church. In living out their marital commitment, husbands and wives share in a unique way in the love of Christ for his Body, the Church, and show to all people the mystery of God's love for his people, the Church. As Christians strive to live out this commitment of love and of the sacred mystery which it signifies, they are strengthened by the grace that comes to them in this sacramental encounter with Christ. Through the sacrament of Matrimony the two people are reborn in the grace of the risen Christ and called to live each day guided by the Spirit of the Lord. By their lives they are witnesses to the redemption that Christ has won for his Church.

In the Old Testament it was important to realize that the marriage of husband and wife was similar to the covenant relationship of God to his people. In the New Testament we must realize that there is a new covenant of love and fidelity between Christ and his Church. The union of husband and wife, as covenant, shares in this new covenant.

Church Teachings

Although it was not until the Council of Florence in the 1430s that the sacramentality of marriage was clearly stated, from the earliest days the Church has always seen that the human institution of marriage should be elevated to the dignity of a sacrament and thus have a special place in the order of grace. At times this has meant defending the value of marriage against those who felt that virginity or perfect chastity were the only acceptable Christian vocations.

It is only in the present century, and especially with the teachings of the Second Vatican Council in the mid 1960s that the dignity of marriage as a sacred calling has clearly been shown. In the same way it is only recently that women have been seen as equal partners with men in the sacrament, and that the two ends of marriage (mutual fulfillment and the procreation of children) have been recognized as equally necessary for a true Christian marriage. Before this, marriage was seen as a calling beneath priesthood or religious life; women were clearly subordinate to men in marriage; and mutual fulfillment was secondary to the goal of procreation.

It is in the *Pastoral Constitution on the Church in the Modern World* (47-52) from the Second Vatican Council where this statement on Christian marriage is made. In this document the Church acknowledges the presence of excessive self-love, worship of pleasure and the illicit practices against human reproduction that are prevalent in the world today. They are aware of the social and psychological factors leading to the attack on proper Christian attitudes toward sexuality, marriage and the family. In light of these factors the Council Fathers try to spell out the ideals of Christian marriage.

The first element to be recognized is that God, as the author of Matrimony, elevated the union of husband and wife beyond the level of human existence.

Thus a man and a woman, who by the marriage covenant of conjugal love 'are no longer two but one flesh' (Mt 19:6) render mutual help and service to each other through an intimate union of their persons and their actions . . . . This authentic married love is caught up into divine love and is governed and enriched by Christ's redeeming power and the saving activity of His Church (48).

This love leads the spouses closer to God and to each other. It strengthens them in their duties as husband and wife, as mother and father. This intimate union also imposes the need for total fidelity on the couple and demands that their union remain unbroken.

The married couple is encouraged to nourish and develop their marriage by pure conjugal love and undivided affections.

Such love, merging the human with the divine, leads the spouses to a free and mutual gift of themselves, a gift proving itself by gentle affection and by deed. Such love pervades the whole of their lives. By its generous activity it grows better and grows greater. Therefore it far exceeds mere erotic inclinations. This love is uniquely expressed and perfected through the marital act. The actions within marriage by which the couple are united intimately and chastely are noble and worthy ones. Expressed in a manner which is truly human, these actions signify and promote that mutual self-giving by which the spouses enrich each other (49).

In fulfilling their duties the Christian couple should be open to the grace of the sacrament and should employ all the Christian virtues to carry out their vocation. In this way they give witness to the joy of their Christian marriage and they serve as signs of the presence of Christ in the world today.

Without trying to make any other purpose seem less important, the duty of parents to bring children into the world (if this is possible) is stressed. It is the outgoing love of husband and wife that becomes incarnate in children. As parents they are then to educate their children in the ways of the faith and to guide them to live by Christian moral principles.

Referring again to the dangers present in the world today, the point is made that in Christian marriage there is a great need to safeguard life from the moment of conception and to avoid "methods of regulating procreation which are found blameworthy by the teaching authority of the Church in its unfolding of the divine law" (51).

In response to similar dangers the intimate union of husband and wife, the sacred duties of mothers and fathers, and the basic dignity of the family must be safeguarded against all opposition.

It is true that these are all lofty ideals. In reality no marriage is perfect. The best of marriages has bad days and hard times. Still, each married couple must strive to embody these Christian ideals in their married life. They are to remember that marriage is a call to perfection and holiness. This should lead to the personal, psychological, sexual and spiritual completion of both husband and wife. This most intimate union should be visibly expressed through their daily life so that the married couple becomes a witness to the Resurrection and to the presence of Christ united in love to his people, the Church.

This calling to holiness through marriage is clearly not easy. Remembering that Matrimony is a sacrament, and that because of this the grace and power of Christ are always present to strengthen the couple as they strive to live out their Christian vocation, makes a person willing to try.

III
MARRIAGE AS CEREMONY: SIGN OF CHRIST FOR ALL TO SEE

All people have ceremonies for the public ratification of marriage. In many instances those ceremonies involve religious rituals to emphasize the dignity and the importance of marriage. The wedding ceremony itself has many variations. Generally it takes place in the presence of relatives and friends and is solemnized by a religious functionary. The ceremony marks the beginning of a new family and confers a new status upon the two people.

In the Christian sacrament of Matrimony it is the action of the bride and the groom that accomplishes the sacramental rite. Their presence in the church standing before the congregation and the external manifestation of their consent brings about the symbolic reality of the marriage bond and initiates the sacramental grace of their conjugal union. It is not the priest but the bride and groom themselves who are the ministers of the sacrament of Matrimony.

For most of the sacraments the priest is the minister. It is the hand of the priest that pours the waters of Baptism or confers the sacramental absolution of the sacrament of Reconciliation. In Matrimony, however, the priest is not the minister but only the official witness of the contract.

The essential element in the Rite of Marriage is the consent of the bride and groom who are the ministers of the sacrament. This is followed by the ratification of the priest who serves as the official witness along with the maid (matron) of honor and best man. The blessing of rings, the nuptial blessing and the incorporation of the Rite of Marriage into the context of a Mass arose in the Middle Ages. In 1970 the English translation of the Revised Rite of Marriage was issued. It is this rite which will be described in the following paragraphs.

The celebration of marriage during Mass is to be considered the normal manner of celebrating this sacrament. However for a good reason (as when one of the parties to the marriage is not a Catholic) the sacrament may be celebrated without the Mass. There might even be an occasion (as when one party to the marriage is not baptized) when it would be advisable to celebrate the sacrament without also celebrating the Mass.

Marriage During the Mass

The celebration of marriage during the Mass begins with a procession to the altar. When the bride and groom and the wedding party gather around the altar with the priest, the Mass begins in the usual manner. The readings at Mass (generally one from the Old Testament, a scriptural response, a reading from the New Testament, the Gospel acclamation and the Gospel) are chosen because of their appropriateness for this special occasion. After the Gospel the priest gives a homily drawn from the sacred texts. He speaks about the mystery of Christian marriage, the dignity of wedded love, the grace of the sacrament and the special responsibilities of married people.

It is at this point that the actual Rite of Marriage takes place. It begins with a brief introduction by the priest reminding the couple of the sacredness of the state in life that they are choosing to enter. He then questions them about the freedom of choice, their intended faithfulness to one another, and the acceptance and upbringing of children.

This is followed by the declaration of consent. The priest may question the bride and groom individually after which they each respond, "I do." At many ceremonies, the bride and groom individually recite the complete form of consent. "I (they say their own name), take you (they say the name of their spouse), to be my wife/husband. I promise to be true to you in good times and in bad, in sickness and in health. I will love you and honor you all the days of my life."

Following this exchange of consent between the bride and groom, the priest says, "You have declared your consent before the Church. May the Lord in his goodness strengthen your consent and fill you both with his blessings. What God has joined together, men must not divide."

The actual ceremony of marriage ends with the blessing and exchange of rings and the general intercessions (prayer of the faithful). The Mass then continues as it usually would until after the "Our Father." At that point the priest faces the bride and groom and recites the nuptial blessing. At the Communion of the Mass the bride and groom and the wedding party may receive Communion under both species of bread and wine. At the end of the Mass before blessing the people the priest offers a special blessing for the newlyweds.

Along with the required elements of the Rite of Marriage there are other customs and traditions which may be observed in the marriage ceremony. In many places it is the custom for the bride (or both the bride and groom) to take a bouquet to the shrine of Our Blessed Mother and to pray for Mary's special help in their marriage. A more recent custom is that of lighting the marriage candle. After the consent and exchange of rings the bride and groom light one large candle from two smaller candles which are then extinguished. This one remaining candle is to signify that in marriage the two individuals become one in Christ who is to be the light of their married life.

Marriage Outside the Mass

This service begins with a greeting by the priest and an opening prayer. It is followed by the Liturgy of the Word and the homily just as it would occur during a marriage ceremony taking place in the Mass.

The Rite of Marriage follows the same format listed above. There is the introduction, the questioning by the priest to ascertain the intentions of the couple, the exchange of consent by the bride and groom, the ratification by the priest and the blessing and exchange of rings. The formulas for the nuptial blessing and the prayer of the faithful are combined. The Lord's Prayer is recited and then the priest offers a final blessing.

It is also possible for Communion to be distributed during this ceremony when the situation calls for this. In that case, the Communion rite is inserted into the ceremony after the "Our Father."

Preparation and Participation

Realizing especially what was said at the beginning of this section about how the bride and groom are the actual ministers of this sacrament, it is only right that they should be involved in the preparations of the ceremony. This preparation is made easier by obtaining a booklet that contains all the authorized readings, prayers and blessings. (One inexpensive and helpful booklet would be: *Together for Life,* by Rev. Joseph Champlin, Ave Maria Press. This booklet also offers 28 short commentaries that can serve as preparation for marriage.)

After studying the material the couple should select the readings, nuptial blessings, prayers and preface which they feel to be the most appropriate for their particular situation. At the same time they should meet with the priest who will be officiating and with the musicians and singers who will be involved in the ceremony to plan the other elements that comprise the complete marriage ceremony.

It is also possible that the bride and groom, members of the wedding party, or special friends and relatives can participate in some special way during the ceremony either reading, singing, or by saying the prayer of the faithful or by taking part in the offertory procession.

IV
MARRIAGE AS A WAY OF LIFE:
LIVING AS A CHRISTIAN COUPLE

It might be good before beginning this section to call to mind what was said earlier about marriage as a vocation, a special calling from God through which a person seeks true holiness and Christian perfection. It must also be remembered that marriage is a sign of the covenant love of Christ for his Church. Just as Christ is always present to his Church, he is present each day as the unseen third party to every Christian marriage. The only thing that can drive Christ from a marriage is the deliberate sin of the married couple.

From this it should be clear that the marriage ceremony is just the beginning. The sacramental reality of marriage must be lived out anew each day. The sacramental words of consent are spoken only once but the marriage remains forever. As the newlyweds leave the church on their wedding day they begin the great adventure of the sacrament of Matrimony.

Just as a man's whole life is changed by the reception of Holy Orders, so too is the life of the couple changed who join together in marriage. Whenever a priest preaches, teaches, celebrates the Mass or the sacraments he is fulfilling the duties undertaken in the sacrament of Holy Orders. In a similar way, whenever the person functions as husband or wife, as mother or father, he/she is living out the sacrament of Matrimony. This means that every act of love, great or small, for each other, for their children or for another person who enters into their home is sacramentalized, or made holy.

This sacramental love covers all aspects of married life. Each day as a husband leaves for work he is living the sacrament of Matrimony. His work is sacramental because through this work he supports his family. Even mowing the lawn or carrying out the trash falls within the scope of the sacrament.

It is the same for the wife. All her actions can be part of the living out of the sacrament, part of the growth in holiness that comes through marriage. If the constant routine of cleaning and cooking threatens to sap the strength of the wife, she should remember that these tasks are valuable in the sight of God because they are part of the sacrament of Matrimony. Thus everything in the marriage, except sin, can become a means of grace and holiness.

In actions like this marriage becomes an event of revelation. God reveals his grace and his love when husband and wife make a total commitment to each other, when they are faithful to each other in changing times, when they embrace in sexual union, when they work together to raise up their family. Every marriage can be an occasion for God's self-revelation calling his people to holiness and perfection.

One might ask how God actually reveals himself in marriage or strengthens the couple with his grace. It might be good to realize that each sacrament grants a grace to dispose or move a person to fulfill the duties proper to that sacrament. For example, the sacramental grace of Confirmation strengthens the Christian to live more fully the life of faith. In confession, the grace of God helps the person to be truly sorry for sins as well as to sincerely determine to avoid these sins in the future. In marriage the couple is given help to fulfill the obligations of their life together. The grace of God enables the married couple to live out the ideals which the Bible and the Church teachings have set forth.

The grace of marriage might come as the guidance of the Spirit for a married person struggling to find a job to support the family or as a couple tries to decide where to move or which house to buy. In a time of tension and conflict the special graces of marriage can serve as a light to the mind which suggests a solution to the difficulties. This grace can also be present as a strengthening of the will needed to make the difficult decisions about living out one's Christian life, about family planning, or about imparting proper moral principles to children.

To receive these helps provided by the sacrament of Matrimony one must cooperate with the Lord. Unless the married couple is open to God's self-revelation in their everyday life the grace of the sacrament will remain as an unused talent. It will be as useless as an untapped oil field. On the other hand, the potential for grace in this sacrament is as great as the potential of that same oil field. The couple who cooperates with the Lord in their marriage will find that his grace is always sufficient for the trials and tribulations that might come their way. In this way, the married couple, through the living out of their marital vocation, will truly grow in holiness and in the ways of Christian perfection. They will bring glory to God and show his greatness to all the people they meet. Then at the end of their earthly life they will be prepared to enter into the joy of the heavenly kingdom.

Appendix One:
Mixed-Faith Marriages

Persons who were involved in a mixed-faith marriage that took place before 1960 might remember it to have been a somewhat humiliating experience. They could not have the ceremony in the church. It would take place in a rectory office or some similar location. Then they were permitted to have the ceremony in the church but only at the Communion rail and not in the sanctuary. Most humiliating of all was the declaration that the non-Catholic person had to sign. It stated that he/she would not interfere with the Catholic spouse as that person practiced the faith and that all children would be baptized and raised as Catholics.

In light of the increase in the number of mixed-faith marriages, and especially because of the efforts at ecumenical understanding that have taken place since 1960, the situation has changed for the celebration of a mixed-faith marriage. The marriage is now celebrated around the altar in the church. If the local bishop allows it and if circumstances are favorable, it is possible to have the mixed-faith marriage take place in the context of a nuptial Mass.

The non-Catholic party no longer must sign any statements. Rather, the Catholic party in the marriage states his/her intention to remain a Catholic and to practice the faith. Also a promise must be made to make every effort to see that the children are baptized and educated in the Catholic faith.

It is also possible for the minister of the non-Catholic party to be present for the ceremony in the Catholic church or for the entire ceremony to take place in the church of the non-Catholic party. For more information about this, a person considering a mixed-faith marriage should contact a priest several months before the planned wedding date.

Is there reason for so much concern when two people who practice different religions decide to marry? The concern of the Church stems from the fact that religion is central to the marriage. Religious beliefs should be the source of unity for the husband and wife. The practice of their faith and their love for the Lord should draw them ever closer together. The greater the difference in religion, the greater the potential for problems. When a Catholic and an Orthodox Christian marry the differences are not that serious. When a Catholic and a baptized non-Catholic (Protestant) marry they share their belief in Jesus Christ but their practices and worship are quite different. Between a Catholic and an unbaptized person (Jew, Buddhist, etc.) there are very great differences. The latter person does not recognize Jesus Christ, the center of Christianity, as Catholics do.

Although the Church is well aware of the difficulties that can come to a marriage because of the different religions of the two people, she does not prohibit such marriages. It is clear that each marriage is as different as the people who enter into it. In a mixed marriage the level of faith and the degree to which that faith is practiced, the specific social and cultural situation, and even the personalities of the two individuals will determine the success or failure of that marriage.

In actual fact many mixed-faith marriages can be more grace-filled than the marriages between two Catholics. The different religions that were initially an obstacle in the marriage can make the two people stronger in their faith and in their love for God, for one another, and for their children. They grow in appreciation for the religion of their spouse and also deepen the awareness of their own gift of faith.

The Church has always been aware of the difficulties that can arise in a mixed-faith marriage. Priests are reminded to be aware of this and to help people as they prepare for mixed-faith marriages. Priests should also be available to strengthen and guide the faithful as they live out their vocation to marriage in a mixed-faith marriage.

Appendix Two:
Annulments

For most people in the Church, annulment is a new word for their religious vocabulary. It is a sad fact that some marriages fail. The love that seemed to be present on the wedding day soon fades, only to be replaced by anger and alienation. The intimate union of husband and wife never materialized. The Christian ideals of marriage seem to be out of reach for this particular marriage. An annulment is petitioned for and may be granted.

Does this mean that the Church allows people to end unhappy or unsuccessful marriages? NO! The Church does not condone divorce. Look to Genesis 2:24 where it says that the two must become one flesh, or to Matthew 19:3-9 where Jesus teaches the people about the indissolubility of the marriage covenant. The Church has always taught and will continue to teach that a true Christian marriage must last until death. What God has joined together no person may divide.

It is important to realize that an annulment is NOT a divorce. (However to comply with the laws of the state a civil divorce must be obtained.) An annulment is a declaration by the Church that a man and woman *never* entered into a true

Christian marriage. The effect of the annulment is to say that what looks like a marriage *never* really was a Christian marriage. The two people may have lived together for several years, may have seemed to be happy, and may have had children but never really had a true Christian marriage.

The annulment states that the persons are not bound to this marital relationship since the marriage in question was not a sacramental union. It does not mean that the relationship was entered into with ill will or moral fault. Rather, an annulment is a statement by the Church that the marital relationship fell short of at least one of the elements demanded as essential by the Church for a sacramental marriage.

How can this be? Remember what is required for the marriage to take place. The couple must fully and freely consent to enter into and live out their Christian marriage. They must agree that their marriage will last forever, that it will be with just that one person, and that in their marriage they will welcome children as being sent by God.

Even though they may have given the right answers to the priest's questions and pronounced the formula of consent on their wedding day, were they completely honest in expressing their consent? Were they acting freely and not being forced into the marriage? Were they mentally and morally able to enter into the marital union? Were they sufficiently mature, physically and psychologically, to undertake the duties of Christian marriage? If the answer to any of these questions is "no," then it is possible that a true Christian marriage does not now and has never existed between the two people.

As the pace of society increases, as people move more freely into marriage and especially as the number of marriage failures increases each year, the Church has acted to aid her people. The Church is encouraging greater premarital preparation on the part of the couple. The priest has been reminded of his duty to fully prepare the faithful for the vocation of marriage which they are choosing to enter.

The Church has also recognized the need to minister to those people whose marriages have failed. There are millions of Catholics in the United States who are not able to participate fully in the sacramental life of the Church because of some marital failure. One of the elements in the Church's multifaceted ministry to these people is the increased use of the annulment procedure. Priests have been made more aware of the procedures to be followed. Greater emphasis has been placed on the psychological factors that can enter into the marriage or cause a union to be nonsacramental. The entire process has been expedited. What used to take years and involve correspondence with Rome can now be done in months within the diocesan offices.

If your marriage has failed or if you are in a second marriage and cannot participate fully in the sacramental life of the Church, or if you know someone who is in this situation, make an appointment to see a priest. Explain the situation. If he thinks there are grounds for a possible annulment he will arrange for the preliminary steps to be taken. Testimony will have to be gathered. It will take time to complete the process but if it allows a person to return to the Church or if a civil marriage can be blessed by the Church, it is certainly worthwhile.

Chapter 8
Holy Orders: Sacrament
of Ministerial Priesthood

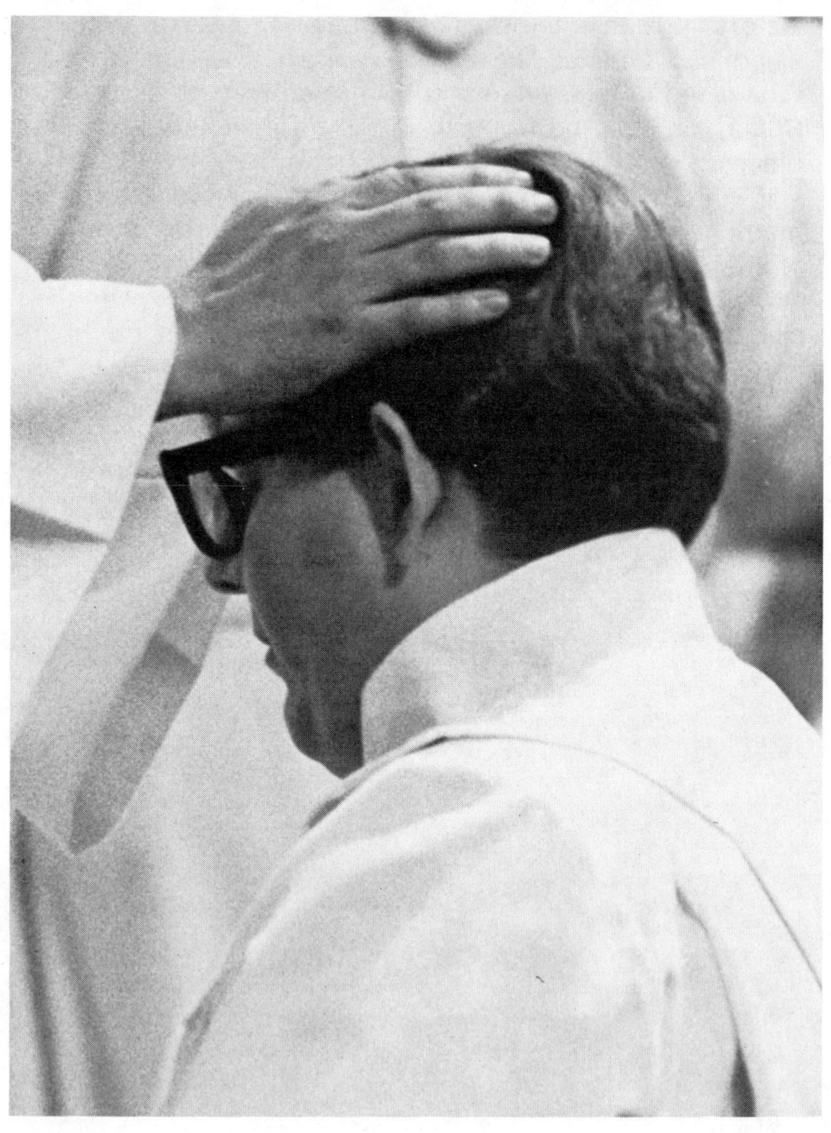

"Dearly beloved people . . . these men, our sons who are your relatives and friends, are about to be raised to the order of priest. You should therefore consider the position in the Church which they will have."

With these words the bishop begins the instructional homily at the Mass of ordination. Continuing, he describes the duties of a priest in the Catholic Church today. He highlights the relationship of the priest to the people whom he is called to serve. He explains to the people that they must cooperate with the priest in the work of salvation.

Speaking to the men being ordained, the bishop reminds them of their priestly responsibilities. They are to preach the Gospel of Jesus Christ and live it in their own lives. Through Baptism they must call all people to salvation. At Mass they renew the sacrifice of Calvary and make Christ present here on earth under the form of bread and wine. They are to be all things to all persons, bringing Christ to each person they meet. Like the apostles of centuries ago, they are called to teach, lead, and sanctify.

This is not an easy task. They are not angels sent from heaven; they are men chosen from among men. "Every high priest is taken from among men and made their representative before God, to offer gifts and sacrifices for sins. He is able to deal patiently with erring sinners, for he himself is beset by weakness and so must take sin offerings for himself as well as for the people" (Heb 5:1-3).

CHRIST THE TRUE PRIEST

St. Paul's letter to the Hebrews (especially chapters 4 to 10) teaches us much about Christ as the true priest. From this description the role of the priest in the Church today can be better understood. It is clear that Christ is the one-and-only true priest. Since Christ's priesthood lasts forever and is unchanging, he must be the model for all priests in every age and in every place. Although Christ is generally seen as Savior, Son of God, Messiah, healer, or teacher, there can be no doubt that he fulfilled the duties of a priest with his death on the Cross.

The Old Testament priests were called upon to offer sacrifice for the people in the Temple. They had an important role in the Jewish community of believers who were awaiting the coming of the Messiah. Melchizedek, the greatest priest of the Old Testament, is regarded as the type or pattern of the priest in today's Church (Gn 14:17-20). But the bread and the wine he offered were just the elements of sacrifice that he chose to offer. It was Christ who transformed the bread and wine into his own body and blood.

The principal duty of the priest has always been to offer sacrifice. In the Old Testament the people would bring their choice animals or the first fruits of their harvest to the Temple at certain times of the year. The priest then would offer sacrifice by killing the animal or burning the harvest offering. This action would be performed so that the people could atone for their sins and be reconciled with God. Thus the priest was the link between God and man in the Old Testament.

Christ came to offer a sacrifice, too. But his was not to offer a choice animal or the first fruits of the harvest. He offered himself on the Cross to the Father so that all people might be reconciled with the Father. Christ was both the victim and the priest. He was the offering and also the offerer. By his death all people could be free from their sins. This was a perfect sacrifice. There can be no greater sacrifice than this: the God-man offering himself totally to the Father through his death on the Cross.

Not only was it a perfect sacrifice, it was the never-ending sacrifice. It happened once on Good Friday at a place called Calvary. Now it goes on forever in eternity affecting all people. Christ by his death brought to completion all the animal and harvest sacrifices of the Old Testament. What those sacrifices lacked because of their strictly human origin Christ completed by his divine sacrifice on the Cross. In the same way, all sacrifices made by people today are completed through the action of Christ offering himself on the Cross.

It is the duty of the priest to offer sacrifice. At Mass, all the faithful offer their sacrifices to the Father. The priest likewise offers his own sacrifices to the Father. These personal sacrifices become pleasing to God when they are joined with the bread and the wine which will be changed into Christ's body and blood. In this action the priest does not offer a totally new and unique sacrifice. He offers the sacrifice of Christ as victim on Calvary, in union with Christ the true High Priest. Each time the priest offers Mass, he becomes one with Christ the true priest and reaches the high point of his priesthood.

THE GOOD SHEPHERD

The priest must also lead and teach the people. As he performs these tasks, he should follow the example of Christ who called himself the Good Shepherd (see Jn 10). Christ was willing to seek out the lost, to care for the sheep in his flock, even to give his life in order to save them. In the ceremony of ordination, the men to be ordained are reminded to be like Christ. They are to remember the example of the Good Shepherd who came to serve rather than to be served, to seek out and save those who had gone astray.

Being like Christ involves many things. A priest can learn much from looking at Christ in action. He preached in words that the people could understand and apply to their lives. He was available when the people needed him. To the sinner he showed mercy and forgiveness. How many times Christ said, ''Your sins are forgiven.'' See the compassion he showed to the woman caught in adultery and to the woman at the well. Christ never ran from the poor, the sick, the maimed, the deranged. Instead, he went to them bringing a message of healing. The blind received a new vision. The deaf heard his word. The dead shared in his new life. He was present with the people in the times of their greatest needs. The priest is called to do these same things.

Being human, Christ knew the sufferings and trials of the people. He knew the temptations that all had to suffer. These realizations allowed him to be present with his healing grace and mercy. In the same way, the priest as a human being is fully aware of the struggles and temptations of this life. He realizes the frailty of human nature. As a priest, he must carry on the healing and saving work of Christ. It is never an easy task for him to do this, but it is possible if he follows the example of Christ, the Good Shepherd.

THE FIRST PRIESTS

In the Gospels there is no clearly defined ceremony of ordination for the apostles. In fact, the word "priest" was not applied to the leaders of the new Church for the first hundred years after Christ. But there can be no doubt that the apostles served the Church as the first priests and bishops. They were closely connected to the work of Christ while he was on earth. They received special instruction, spent much time with him, and saw all the great actions he performed.

The apostles each received a special call to follow Christ, and they responded immediately to his summons. After learning at the feet of the Master, they were sent out to preach and baptize (Mt 10). They were given the power to heal (Mk 6:1-13) and to forgive sins (Jn 20:23). At the Last Supper when our Lord instructed the apostles to "Do this in memory of me," a further extension of their power could be seen. As shepherds of the early believers, they were to preside at the breaking of the bread and to impart to the people what we call sacraments today.

The office of leader in the Christian community passed on from the apostles to their successors. They were to represent the believers and to be a sign of Christ's presence within the community. There must be a connecting link between the people who are designated as leaders and the rest of the people in the Church. History shows that there were times in the Church when too much stress was placed on the role of the priests and bishops, thus obscuring the role of the faithful. At other times, however, the role of the faithful has loomed so large that the specific function of ordained priests and bishops has been overshadowed.

THE UNIVERSAL PRIESTHOOD

In the early Church it was very clear that all baptized believers shared in the priesthood of Christ. "You are a chosen race, a royal priesthood, a people set apart to sing the praises of God who called you out of darkness into his wonderful light" (1 Pt 2:9). All who believed were baptized. They then gave witness to the faith and to the presence of Christ in the pagan world. All members of the Christian community had essential tasks to perform.

The early Church was very much aware of the power of the Spirit — as seen in her choice of leaders and the gifts bestowed on her members. As promised by Christ, the Holy Spirit imparted many special gifts at the first Pentecost. The early Christians recognized and made use of the different charisms, or services, that contributed to the building up of the priestly community. Some could preach or teach. Others could heal, work miracles, or prophesy. Still others could speak in tongues or discern the Spirit (1 Cor 12). But there had to be someone to direct this community of believers which began spreading to all points of the known world.

The leaders were chosen especially to preach and teach. Their office was signified by the imposition of hands and the calling down of the Holy Spirit. Paul recalls Timothy's ordination in the Spirit: "That is why I am reminding you now to fan into a flame the gift that God gave you when I laid hands on you. God's gift was not a spirit of timidity, but the Spirit of power, and love, and self-control" (2 Tm 1:6-7). Everyone could proclaim the Word and witness to the faith, but only the ordained leader had the power to preach in the assembly, to lead the Eucharist, and to guide the community.

As the Church continued to expand, the role of the priest became more important. Often he was the only educated — or best educated — person in the community, and because of this he was called upon to do most everything in the Church. The lay people were allowed to do less and less. The priests and bishops became a special class in the Church.

In the 1500s, Martin Luther and the reformers reacted to this separation of priest and people. They revived the idea that all those baptized shared in the priesthood of Christ. But in doing so they greatly lessened the original authority of the priest and denied that Holy Orders was a sacrament. To rectify this, the Council of Trent (1551) reaffirmed that there is an external, visible priesthood in the Church. Christ himself instituted the sacrament of Holy Orders. It was the duty of the officially ordained priest to celebrate the Mass and officiate at the sacraments.

But Trent's decrees led to an even further separation between priest and people. With the reaffirmation of the original authority of the priest and the renewed declaration on the sacramentality of the priesthood, the doctrine of universal priesthood fell into abeyance. The clerical state thus became institutionalized. And this was the situation until the Second Vatican Council was convened by Pope John XXIII in 1962.

During the sessions of the Council the assembled Fathers considered the role of the ordained priest in the world today. They noted that the priest's chief responsibility is to bring about the presence of Christ in the Church and to share in Christ's office as teacher, sanctifier, and leader. He is chosen to act as mediator between God and man. The Council went on to list some of his essential duties. He is to preach the Gospel, give pastoral service to the faithful, and celebrate the Mass and the sacraments. The official priesthood is to be distinct from the priesthood of the faithful "in essence and degree." The powers of priesthood are conferred through the sacrament of Holy Orders.

In making this distinction, however, the Council pointed out that every effort must be made to realize the priesthood of all the faithful. There is a great need today as in the days of the early Church to spread the Gospel in a pagan world. All people need to hear the Good News of salvation and to experience the presence of Christ in their lives. This can only come about through the common effort of all persons baptized into the universal priesthood working along with the ordained priests.

"For their part, the faithful join in the offering of the Eucharist by virtue of their priesthood. Likewise, they exercise that priesthood by receiving the sacraments, by prayer and thanksgiving, by the witness of a holy life, and by self-denial and active charity" (*Dogmatic Constitution on the Church,* 10).

THREE LEVELS OF HOLY ORDERS

Most people think of Holy Orders in terms of priesthood. But a deacon also receives this sacrament. Priesthood is really the second level of Holy Orders. The bishop, at his consecration, receives the fullness of the sacrament. Before looking at the steps leading to ordination and the actual ceremony, it might be good to consider the development of each order together with its duties and responsibilities.

Deacon

It is the order of deacon, and not priest or bishop, that receives the most attention in the pages of the New Testament. The election of seven men from the community is noted in chapter six of Acts. The apostles pray over the candidates that the Spirit might come to them. Then they lay hands on the men as a sign of their entrance into the order of deacon. The deacons are instructed to assist the apostles as they serve the people. It is quite clear that the deacons are to be strong believers, upright Christians, and men dedicated to the service of the community and the spread of the Gospel (see Tm 3:8-13). It was the deacon Stephen who is remembered as the first person to give his life as a martyr for the Church.

As the importance of the bishop and the priest grew, the importance of the deacon diminished. For centuries the diaconate was the last step on the road to priesthood. In his last years of training, the seminarian passed through the various minor orders. With a fitting ceremony he was installed as an acolyte, lector, porter, exorcist, and subdeacon. Although these were not sacraments, they were definite signs of position in the Church. A seminarian would be ordained deacon a few months before his ordination to the priesthood.

Recently there has been a renewed emphasis on the order of deacon. A seminarian is ordained to the diaconate and serves as a deacon for a period of time (often six months to a year or more) before his ordination to the priesthood.

Even more significant than the renewed emphasis on the diaconate for seminarians who are to be ordained priests is the renewal of the permanent diaconate. It is now possible for a mature married man to enter a program of study in order to become a deacon. He is to work with the bishop and his priests serving the People of God in the ministries of the liturgy, the Word, and charity. With the permission of his bishop, the deacon can baptize, distribute the Eucharist, assist at marriages, bring Communion to the dying, and officiate at funerals. He leads the people in prayer, reads the Scriptures, preaches, and teaches. In a word, he serves the People of God working in the image of Christ and following the example of those first deacons in the early Church.

Bishop

The office of bishop in the Church can be traced back to Christ who personally instituted this position in the Church. It was not immediately clear, however, just what his function was to be. As a direct successor to the apostles he held much power. Gradually it became clear how this power would be used. By the year 110 history shows the bishop serving as head of the local church. He was seen as the representative of Christ and the image of God the Father. It was the bishop who celebrated the Eucharist. He was also the one to guarantee the unity of the Church in a specific area and to insure the harmony of his believers with those throughout the Church.

Bishops succeed the apostles both in historical lineage and in relation to their position in the Church. A further link is seen between bishops and Christ. They are related to Christ as closely as the apostles were to Jesus when he walked the earth.

A bishop has many important duties. As the principal teacher in his diocese he sees to it that the truths of the Catholic faith and the principles of morality are correctly taught. As first among preachers, he speaks in the name of Christ. He governs the people as the vicar of Christ. In his own diocese, the bishop is clearly the head of the Church. He does not possess total authority, however. All the bishops of a country come together to set practice and policy to be followed in their land. All the bishops of the world form a "college" or united group by virtue of their being successors to the apostles. Even in this group the bishops do not possess total authority. The decisions of individual bishops, local groups of bishops, and even the world-wide body of bishops are subject to the authority of the principal bishop, the Pope.

Priest

The Church has always had a priesthood. However, there was a time in the earliest days of the Church when there was no office of priest as it is known today. There were bishops and deacons, elders and people appointed to various ministries in the Church, but no priests. The office arose as the number of believers began to grow to such numbers that the bishop was no longer able to care for their needs properly.

This developed at the beginning of the second century. The priest ranked between the deacon and the bishop. He was ordained to function in the name of the bishop. His duties were to preach and sanctify. It was his privilege to lead the people in prayer and at the Eucharist.

The same relationship between the two exists today. When the priest preaches, teaches, or offers the sacrifice of the Mass, he does so in the name of the bishop. Both share in the priesthood of Christ. As such they work together for the good of the people and the building up of the Church.

The activities of today's priest fall into three basic categories. First, he is called to preach by word and action. His message should bring people the Good News of salvation and lead them to conversion, renewal, and growth. Secondly, he is the leader of worship. He represents Christ performing the actions of salvation for the community. In doing this he becomes a sign of Christ's presence among the people and stands between God and them as a mediator of the new covenant. Thirdly, he is to be a leader. Taking the image of the good shepherd, he gives himself to the people of his Church and the world.

VOCATION

A man does not become a priest overnight. It takes many long years of study. But before this there has to be a divine call. Without this call, or vocation, a man can never become a priest. The Bible records dozens of cases where the Lord vividly and clearly called a man to his service. Moses found the Lord calling him from the burning bush (Ex 2). The boy Samuel heard the voice of the Lord in the night (1 Sm 3). Isaiah received his call during a heavenly vision (Is 6). Jeremiah debated his call with the Lord. He lost the debate and became a prophet (Jer 1). The apostles dropped whatever they were doing when they heard the call to "Come and follow me" (Mk 1:16; 2:13). St. Paul was knocked to the ground by a light from the sky (Acts 9).

Ask any priest about his call to the priesthood. Very few can tell of a call that would match those recorded in the Bible. Most priests felt an inner calling to serve God and man in a better way. Hearing the call they went to a seminary in order to start their education for the priesthood and determine whether God has really called them.

SEMINARY TRAINING

Before his ordination a man spends many years studying in seminaries. If a young man feels that he has a calling to be a priest, he can begin his training immediately after elementary school. A high school seminary teaches much the same courses as any high school that has a program of preparation for college. Once in college the seminarian is expected to pursue a liberal arts education. He centers his efforts on philosophy, theology, and the social sciences needed for his ministry as a priest. After college, he studies an additional four years of theology. At this time he concentrates on the basic truths of the Church, the Bible, morality, sacraments, and Church history. There are also courses in preaching, liturgy, and Church law.

Throughout the training for the priesthood great emphasis is placed on spiritual development. The seminarian learns that the priest must be a man of prayer if he is to succeed in his ministry. Through personal and group prayer, by daily Mass and the sacraments, and in reading and reflection, he learns to center his life on the person of Christ.

The seminarian must also undertake a program of priestly service during his years in the seminary. Just as he must learn from the classroom courses, the seminarian must learn to function as a priest serving his people. This service can take many forms. Among other things, seminarians teach religion classes in the CCD program, conduct adult education classes, visit hospitals and homes for the aged. Their work should fill a need in the Christian community and also serve as a training program for future priests.

ORDINATION

The long years of study come to a fitting conclusion with the ceremony of ordination. The bishop presides at the ceremony. The Mass begins as usual. After the Gospel the names of the candidates are called. Each one responds by saying, "I am ready and willing." Their superiors testify that the men are indeed ready for ordination. The bishop accepts this testimony and the congregation shows their approval in an appropriate manner. In the United States, applause can be a very moving sign of approval.

The ceremony of ordination continues with the instruction given by the bishop. This homily centers on the duty of the priest and his place in the Christian community. It is followed by an examination of the candidates. The bishop asks the candidates if they will care for the Lord's flock, celebrate the sacred mysteries for the sanctification of the faithful, preach the Gospel, explain the faith, and give their lives to bring people to salvation. Each candidate then comes forward to pledge his obedience to the bishop. Next, the bishop asks the people to join in praying the Litany of the Saints. The candidates lie prostrate on the floor while everyone else kneels.

Next follows the essential element of the sacrament. One by one the candidates kneel before the bishop. Saying nothing, the bishop lays his hands on the head of each candidate. After this, all the priests present impose their hands on the head of each candidate. (From New Testament times the laying on of hands has been a sign for ordination. It has signified the calling down of the Holy Spirit with his special graces of priesthood.) Then the bishop stretches out his arms and prays the prayer of consecration. With these two actions (the laying on of hands and the prayer of consecration) the candidates have become priests.

The newly ordained priests put on the stole and chasuble for the first time. Dressed as priests they go before the bishop who anoints their hands with sacred oil. (From earliest times, anointing has been the sign of election by God to a special office.) After this anointing the new priest goes before the bishop to touch the chalice, the paten, and the host. It is with these sacred vessels and the elements of bread and wine that he will best serve the people by offering sacrifice to God. The ceremony of ordination ends with the bishop and all the priests giving the sign of peace to each of the newly ordained priests. This is a sign that they are welcome as sharers in the ordained priesthood of Jesus Christ. After the ceremony of ordination has been completed the Mass resumes at the offertory with the newly ordained priests concelebrating their first Mass with the bishop.

CONCLUSION

A priest never forgets the day of his ordination, yet it is only the beginning. He is now a priest forever. He has received the sacrament of Holy Orders. As a priest, he is now to go forth and dedicate his life to the service of all people by imitating Christ, the true priest.

This service of the People of God is clearly indicated in the *Decree on the Ministry and Life of Priests.* He is ordained for "the service of Christ, the Teacher, the Priest, and the King." He serves the people through ministry of the Word, ministry of the sacraments and the Eucharist, and ministry of leadership. And the "source and summit" of these functions rests in the Eucharist. His is the privilege to form a community with a deep sense of its own identity (the local church), but one that remains open in love and action to the wider community of the whole Church and the world. His purpose will be to help men and women grow to full Christian maturity.

He will be known by the way he lives. And the success of his priesthood will depend very much on his humble obedience, his perfect continence, and his spirit of detachment from material goods together with his sense of poverty.

The second of these virtues — perfect continence or celibacy — has been challenged in modern times. But the true priest will answer the cries for optional celibacy with the words of the Council: "Through celibacy observed for the sake of the kingdom of heaven (see Mt 19:12), priests are consecrated to Christ in a new and distinguished way. They more easily hold fast to him with undivided heart (see 1 Cor 7:32-34). They more freely devote themselves in him and through him to the service of God and men. They more readily minister to his kingdom, and to the work of heavenly regeneration, and thus become more apt to exercise paternity in Christ, and do so to a greater extent" *(Priests,* 16).

As Father Terence Tierney writes in his booklet *Should You Become a Priest?* (Liguori Publications, Liguori, MO 63057):

"Celibacy is not a sacrifice but a grace, not a duty but a privilege, not a crucifixion but a divine blessing; it is not the only form of a divine call but a special one. Priestly celibacy finds its origin in the Jesus story, not in the interpretation of that story down through the ages in conciliar statements and canonical definitions. The reason the celibacy issue is so pointed results from the fact that men have grounded its birth at the Council of Trent instead of at Bethlehem, have remained steadfast to juridical aspects and forgotten the Bible" (p. 47).

Lord, send workers into your vineyard! Give your Church holy priests!

More Basic Help on the Subject of Sacraments

Leader's/Teacher's Guide
for THE SACRAMENTS TODAY

A practical, well-written guide to help teachers or discussion group leaders in using THE SACRAMENTS TODAY. $2.95

Worksheets for THE SACRAMENTS TODAY

Excellent for classroom use OR discussion groups. The worksheets are bound in sets in booklet form — a neat convenient accompaniment to this book and/or the Leader's/Teacher's Guide.

Set of 30 worksheets in booklet form — $1.50

Will Religion Make Sense to Your Child?
by Earnest Larsen and Patricia Galvin
Helpful preparation for first Communion

Presents to adults some new emphases on creation and original sin, redemption, sacraments, Baptism, Penance, and the Eucharist. The second half of the book suggests ways to introduce the material to children with stories, activities, and questions. $1.95

Helping Your Child Know Right from Wrong
A Redemptorist Pastoral Publication
Helpful preparation for first Confession

This book presents basic understandings of conscience, sin, and forgiveness. Part ONE is written *to* and *for* adults. Part TWO takes the themes presented on the adult level and weaves them into stories, questions, and activities that parents and teachers can use to help children prepare for the sacrament of Reconciliation. $2.50

Helping Your Child Appreciate the Mass
and the Sacraments
by Thomas Artz, C.SS.R., and Ruth Marie Haley, S.S.N.D.

This book shows parents how to begin IN THE HOME to introduce children to the Mass and the sacraments as celebrations — and to weave their meaning into the fabric of family life. $2.95